Dressing My
Inner Beauty
Journal

TaSheekia Perry

Contact Information:

Tasheekia Perry
Address P.O Box 43
Lehigh Acres, Fl. 33970
Phone: 1-888-364-0002
Email: cdfs2006@yahoo.com
Website Address: www.cdfs2006.com

Publication:

ISBN: 978-0-9753857-8-4
Printed in the United States of America First Edition Printing: August 2017© 2017 by Crowning Daughters for Success, Inc. All Rights Reserved.

Sozo Omnimedia

Content editing by: Martha Clare Brinkman and Danielle Viens-Payne
Book Layout by Samuel Okike (Psalmyy on Fiverr).

Foreword

TaSheekia is a ladies lady and a role model for the next generation of ladies. I know her as family and as a friend. Her mom has been my best friend for years. But more than anything, I know TaSheekia by her spirit. What she has to impart to young ladies needs to be bottled up and given to every community. The contents of that bottle will be priceless. Preparation is one of golden keys to productive living. Most of our teen girls have been prepared to maintain a great outward image, but have not been prepared inwardly to take on life's issues. The primary goal of teen years is to be prepared for adulthood and have a sense of confidence and independence to live a life of purpose. Many teen girls face various potholes that prevent them from exuding confidence, choosing healthy relationships, using the power in their voice, making quality decisions, and so many more characteristics needed to stay above the waters of life.

Many times adults forget about the pressures of fitting in, the unrealistic expectations of media, and the difficulties of maneuvering through life as a young girl. The difference between what many adults faced as teens and what today's teens are facing now is simply access and exposure. Today's girls are exposed to a lot more, and they have access to more because of the progression of technology and media. This access can either equip them for success or hinder their success.

The information in this Journal is directed toward any young girl who desires to embrace the true essence of herself, make a positive impact and maintain a balanced level of confidence without compromising who God created her to be. Are you ready for this amazing journey? This Dressing My Inner Beauty Journal will not make any choices for you. It is a wonderful map filled with valuable information, inspiring stories, and biblical principles that will surely assist any young girl on their journey of life.

Love you Sheekia,

Apostle Kimberly Daniels

Dedication

This Dressing My Inner Beauty Journal is dedicated to You and everyone who planted a seed of encouragement and inspired me to be my best self. Thank you for selflessly imparting into me, my vision and my spirit. A very special thanks to the number one woman in my life- my mom! I am forever grateful to God for entrusting such a life- changing project into my hands.

About the Author

TaSheekia Perry, originally from Jacksonville, but now living in Fort Myers, FL, had a humble upbringing and faced many challenges while growing up on public assistance. Not having the finances or resources to achieve her own goals deepened her faith and gave her the strength to overcome life's obstacles.

Perry attended Florida Agricultural and Mechanical University(FAMU) in Tallahassee and worked her way into a position traveling across the USA for photo shoots and modeling competitions. From 1996 to 2002, she appeared in several national and local hairstyle magazines and later directed modeling classes and conducted make-up artistry for the Barbizon Modeling School, Sears Model's Club, and The Studio on the Gulf.

Overcoming many obstacles and life experiences has given Perry the ability to encourage positive growth in the lives of others. She has worked with youth and adults for over 12 years in the areas of healthy self-esteem, self-image, and proper social etiquette. Her enrichment program *Crowning Daughters for Success* is taught in Lee County Public Schools, the Boys & Girls Club of Collier County, Our Mother's Home, and various other youth organizations.

Perry has been featured on several TV news programs and in local magazines. She has won multiple awards for her work with the youth of Southwest Florida. The CDFS Program was awarded the Lee Pitts Live Youth Education of the Year and the Boys & Girls Club Florida Area Council Program Excellence Award for Character and Leadership Development. She is a regular on *Lee Pitts Live,* a local talk show, where she has the opportunity to reach young girls and women with a positive message. She recently launched *Girl Talk,* a mini-segment on *Lee Pitts Live,* which motivates, directs, and creates awareness through relatable topic discussions and interviews. She is currently conducting a statewide Inner-Beauty Campaign for middle and high school girls, and has published her *Crowning Daughters for Success Life Manual.* The campaign and manual will assist young girls in embracing the true essence of beauty and will empower them to make a difference in life by reinforcing core values and positive character traits.

Perry is also an ordained minister with over 15 years of experience. She uses multiple platforms and venues to motivate, equip, and liberate others. Whether she is involved in speaking engagements, seminars, or one-on-one coaching, Perry is in the business of transforming lives for the better. If you would like to join the CDFS Pitch In Project, sign up a daughter, or implement this program at your organization, please visit the CDFS website to stay updated www.cdfs2006.com.

Table of Contents

Letter to the Beauty!

*C*rowning Daughters for Success is an enrichment program developed with You in mind. This Journal was designed to help adolescent girls like you discover their personal best through character development, value exploration, goal setting, self-esteem building, and, most importantly, scripture. Through this journal, you will have the opportunity to share your feelings and anxieties, discover the common challenges of growing up, explore the value of diversity, and examine and develop your own personal values **without being judged**. The D.M.I.B. Journal will provide solutions to "real world" problems using time-tested Biblical principles. As a teen, it is imperative for you to develop your own moral compass which will be critical for your future success. You can have confidence in yourself without compromising your values.

This Journal will also teach the value of courtesy, etiquette, proper care of one's body and mind, and help to develop positive social interaction. It is my desire to see the positive outcomes of girls bonding and working productively together. It is strongly encouraged that you invite another Beauty to take this Inner Beauty Journey with you. Please read each topic at your own pace, and share in the journal entries how you Dressed your Inner Beauty. For example: My brother ate my favorite snack. I was so angry and wanted to react negatively. I dressed My Inner Beauty by remaining positive, when I wanted to lose my cool.

This journal will encourage self-exploration and self-expression. Let the Inner Beauty Journey Begin!

TaSheekia Perry,

Author and Founder of Crowning Daughters for Success Enrichment Program

Dressing My Inner Beauty

The Power of Girls Bonding is the Latest Fashion!

Welcome to the best journey you could ever embark on. It is imperative that you take this opportunity and get to know yourself, share your experiences with others, and just bond! **Girls bonding is something very special and needed**. We don't see a lot of bonding among women in media, families, or communities. I believe that when girls begin to bond and establish codes and standards to live by, they can have more laughs, genuine support, empowerment, and less drama. Drama seems to be the latest trend among girls and women. The majority of TV shows that star women in lead roles start out as if they are going to stick together through thick and thin. However, before the first commercial break they are stabbing each other in the back, pulling hair, and ending friendships. Why? Drama boosts ratings and in return increases salaries. Our girls see too much drama among women who should be models of what class, authenticity, and productivity should look like. Many girls are mimicking these negative behaviors because they have been accepted by the majority to camouflage feelings of hurt, disappointment and the human desire to "fit in".

To strengthen and promote authentic bonding among girls, try implementing the following **TaSheekia's Tidbits**:

- Authentic bonding promotes healthy friendships and allows them to form.

- When healthy friendships are formed, girls establish a strong support system among themselves.

- No matter who you are, everyone desires support and encouragement. When girls bond, they are able to share experiences, hold each other accountable, and assist each other in becoming their best selves.

- Authentic bonding alleviates negative competition and causes girls to inspire each through their special talents, similarities, and differences.

- Loyalty is established when authentic connections take place. Girls bonding allows them to be true to themselves and to each other.

- Encouraging other young girls to bond will assist in eliminating bullying, self-hate, and negative attitudes toward each other.

- Sisterhood is a key connection that will lead to productivity, authenticity, and an unbreakable bond among girls!

Scriptures to Think About

Please open your bible and read one of my favorite stories about Women Bonding.

The Book of Ruth will help you understand, embrace and apply the principles of Bonding.

Please write notes about the Bonding Experience of Ruth and Naomi.

_____

_____

_____

_____

_____

_____

_____

_____

_____

_____

_____

_____

_____

_____

_____

_____

_____

Dressing My Inner Beauty Journal Page
How I Dressed My Inner Beauty Today

_____

_____

_____

_____

_____

_____

_____

_____

_____

_____

_____

_____

_____

_____

_____

_____

_____

_____

_____

Monday   Tuesday   Wednesday   Thursday   Friday   Saturday   Sunday

Dressing My Inner Beauty
What I Think of Me is the Latest Fashion!

The Power of Healthy Self Esteem

The word **self-esteem** is very powerful. I'm pretty sure that you have heard it before, but you've probably never thought about what it had to do with you. **Self-esteem is how a person feels about him or herself.** It's how much you value yourself, and how important you think you are. This is the ONLY time it's all about you. Yes, girlfriend! **Self-esteem is how YOU feel about YOU**—not how your friends, pets, teachers, neighbors, or even family members feel about you.

Now, many things can influence how we feel about ourselves. The things people say to us and the things that happen in our lives can have a great deal of influence on how we feel about ourselves; but in the end, it is how you feel about yourself that is important.

Sometimes you may have negative feelings about yourself because of negative things others have said about you, or because of negative experiences you have been through. Here is some GOOD NEWS! When God created you, he created a **masterpiece**, and the only thing that really matters is how God feels about you and how you feel about you.

God thought enough to create you, so that settles the question, "Who Loves You?" **You are loved dearly**. It is important for you to know and understand the power of healthy self-esteem so that you will not allow anything to stand in the way of being proud of whom God has created you to be. There are two ways you can choose to feel about yourself: You can feel **good** about yourself or you can feel **bad** about yourself. Whichever way you choose will lead you on your journey to having either a healthy or an unhealthy self-esteem. Brace yourself! I have worked with many young girls ages seven and older, and I have thought of them as beautiful, smart, talented, FAB young ladies. Sadly though, a lot of them did not feel about themselves the way God feels about them, nor did they see themselves the way I saw them. They were always talking down and thinking negatively about themselves. Speaking or thinking negatively about yourself all the time can eventually cause you to make poor choices.

For example, I knew of a beautiful young girl that always compared herself to others. She never had anything kind to say about herself. She was very talented in drawing and creating beautiful art projects. Everyone else noticed how nice, smart, and talented she was, but she would not believe it. Eventually, she stopped using her talents in fear of being considered LAME, and started goofing off in school to gain attention from the so-called "popular clique". Her grades went down and she began to get into a lot of trouble.

Now, I want you to think for a moment about that popular, yet mean, girl at your school. She is beautiful and nicely dressed, but hurts others. She is bossy and only cares about herself. When we look at her outward appearance, we would say she has a healthy self-esteem.

NEWS FLASH! Her self-esteem is just as low and un-healthy as the girl who is always speaking negatively about herself. Unhealthy self-esteem is not concerned with color, age, or gender. It sticks to people who have a hard time accepting and loving themselves for who they are—people who don't understand how special God made them.

Having a healthy self-esteem is all about knowing that without Jesus, you are nothing. Therefore, without Him you will have a hard time feeling good about yourself in a healthy way. **You were made in HIS image, and are considered a valuable and beautiful individual to HIM.** When you realize that it is Jesus who makes you the FAB princess you are, you can feel good about yourself, and look the part, too.

It is sad that even some adults misjudge whether or not a young person has healthy self-esteem. We as adults see you all jazzed up, looking like you are enjoying life and not having any problems. In reality, many of you are going through so many difficult things within. It is important for everyone to know that healthy self-esteem starts from within and then works its way out.

Think about how you look in the mirror on the first day of school, when you are wearing your new FAB outfit. You say to yourself, "Now I look good! I bet nobody has this outfit." You feel confident and good about yourself until you get to school and see another girl wearing the same outfit as yours. She is even getting more compliments, and it seems that no one is noticing you or what you are wearing. You begin to doubt yourself, and you start to feel down and may even feel a little angry.

This happens to the best of us when we forget what is really important. Wearing the latest fashions, being a part of popular cliques, or knowing how many boys admire you is not important. Are you ready for this? You are not going to hear this on your favorite TV show, in the latest music, or even in conversation among your friends, but here we go. **An important nugget about healthy self-esteem is that it is all about being the best you can be.** Enjoy every moment of your journey to becoming a better person from the inside out.

When you have a healthy self-esteem, you are able to have a positive opinion of yourself WITHOUT being conceited, and without bragging about how great you are. It's more like quietly knowing that you're worth a lot—**priceless, in fact**! It's not about thinking you're perfect—because nobody is perfect—but knowing that you're worthy of being loved and accepted. Yes, You! You are worthy of being loved and accepted". With healthy self-esteem, you realize you must be careful about comparing yourself to others. Sometimes this can make you feel good or even inspire you to improve in some way, but other times it can make you overlook what's truly good about yourself and cause you to feel bad.

Enjoy the process of becoming a better person according to **God's standards**. It is a process because it will take time to discover what your strengths and weaknesses are. Remember, having healthy self-esteem is not about being perfect. Therefore, the way you feel about and carry yourself should not be based on living a PERFECT life. For example, I am a very good singer in the shower! Well, let's just say I will stick to the shower—{LOL}. I can take a million singing lessons, yet may never have the voice to sing a solo…well, maybe so low that no one can hear me—Ha! I do, however, have a gift from God to encourage people and make them feel better. I am also gifted to do other things, but singing is just not one of them. I accept that about myself and love myself anyway. You can too. The shower will always be my stage and the shampoo bottle my blinged out mic!

Speaking in front of large crowds may not be one of your strengths, but playing an instrument in front of a large crowd may be. This is not to say that you should give up on everything you feel you are not good at doing. Try and try again at anything you want to succeed in. Take positive risks. If you find you are weak in an area, don't beat yourself up about it or be jealous of the next person who may have the strengths you seek. You do not get an "excuse ticket" when it comes to your attitude, behavior, or education. With dedication, practice, and dependence on God for help, you can succeed in these areas with no problem. Let's make a deal—no more sitting in the room all alone thinking negatively about yourself. What you think about yourself will affect some very important parts of your life. Yep! It can affect your value system (what you think is right or wrong), your attitude, and even your choice of friends.

Wow! What you think about yourself affects a lot of things. I know sometimes you wonder, "What is wrong with me? Why can't I just be different? Why won't certain people hang out with me?" At times, things look like they're going wrong, and sometimes we feel like we are wearing a big sign on our back that says "DO NOT TALK

TO ME BECAUSE I'M LAME". Guess what? If you start to think more positively about yourself, and realize you are not perfect, and that not everyone is going to like you or be your best friend, regardless of the reasons, you will quickly see for yourself that life is not over. You can concentrate on your strengths, enjoy the people who do love you, and keep being the best YOU that you can be!

It is so important—if you are going to be SUCCESSFUL, you must think SUCCESSFUL. This means you must turn that "stinking thinking" into "positive thinking". Here is a **golden nugget**—most people who think negatively about themselves and their lives have a very difficult time keeping positive relationships. You are a valuable gem. Yes, you are more valuable than the biggest diamond anyone could find. As you begin to discover the treasure within yourself, nothing will be able to stop you.

I want to take you on a spiritual field trip to show you why you should shout out the **Praise**, "Thank you, God, for creating me!" **When God created humans, he created us with one purpose in mind—to be in His image and to have a relationship with Him.** His image is His spirit that abides inside each and every one of us who believes in Jesus. You know people judge us based on what image we portray. Most people think we are hip if we wear the latest brands or think we are popular if we have certain friends. Well, people also know if you love and respect God. They can see you are wearing His image, which is **Righteousness**. His image is not black or white, straight hair or locks, Name Brand shoes or Name Brand Attire. He created us to look like Him in our **CHOICES** and **ATTITUDE** so that we could bring honor to Him.

I know you see pretty, popular girls all around you, but I want you to know that there is something so special about you that no one can compete with. The most amazing thing about you is that there is only **ONE** you. So, the next time you look in the mirror and want to think negatively about yourself, or are afraid to walk into a room with confidence, or you fear going somewhere because your clothes or hair may not be like everyone else's, remember that **God created us uniquely different but equally beautiful from the inside out.** Our fingerprints prove that we are all an original design by God's own hands.

Wait! Someone still does not understand! What does **original** mean? It means the first; the real thing; unique; creative; not a copy. And if you look up anything that is of importance, you will find that the original is worth more than a copy any day. For example, an original document has more importance than a copy. If I wanted to go on a cruise and only had a copy of my birth certificate, they would not accept the copy. I would have to order an original because that would be the only proof that it was real.

Most girls are into purses, and if you thought you were buying an original name brand purse, you would be disappointed to find out it was a copy. Because no matter how closely the copy and the original resemble each other, the original would be sturdier and more durable than the copy. The copy would be made out of a cheaper material and not last as long.

You are the "Real Thing, Baby". Be the best you that God created you to be. To be unique, but equal at the same time, is great. If we were all created the same, there would be no variety of shapes, color, or sizes. **Variety** makes our world an exciting place to live in. Imagine wearing blue every day of the week, or eating spaghetti for dinner every night, or having the same routine every day without any changes. YUCK!

We were created to be different because God knew that we would have different likes and dislikes. Despite all of the differences we may have, the Bible tells us that EVERTHING God created was considered GOOD. When God sees us, He does not rate us on a scale from 1-10. It is so like Him to find a 10 in all He created because **He can't create less than the best**. Sometimes when we create something, we make mistakes and have to start all over again until we are satisfied with our masterpiece. Well, not God! He took one look at His creation and said, "This is all GOOD."

It is so easy to look at another person's life and see something you might not have and take for granted what you do have. One of the devil's biggest tricks is to make you feel like you are not good enough by looking at someone else. Before you know it, you have fallen into the "Self-Pity Pit"—feeling down, talking down and looking down on the perfect 10 God created you to be.

Not only are our thoughts powerful, our tongues are powerful as well. You must decide at this point in your life that what you think and say about yourself will not be based on what you have, where you live, how many friends you have, what type of family you come from, or on the images you see on TV. What you think and say about yourself should be based on the fact that you were created by hands that make no- mistakes. Hands of an all-powerful, all knowing, and loving God.

Now if that does not make you blush, I don't know what will. So, what do you have to lose by being proud and feeling good about being you? It is way too easy to focus on those **"terrible toos"**...I'm too fat, I'm too skinny, I'm too poor, my mom is too strict, I have too many problems...Remember to focus on your strengths. These are the things that you are good at and the things that make a positive difference in your life and the lives of those around you.

If there are things you need to change for the better, don't get discouraged if you don't get it the first time around. Keep striving to be the best you. You are going to need help on your journey. This is why the Bible tells us that when we receive Jesus in our hearts, He gives us His Spirit, the **Holy Spirit. This is the Spirit of God who lives inside of us**. Now who couldn't be their best with the Holy Spirit living inside them? He gives us the power to do what we feel we can't do and encourages us to be what others say we can't be.

This is helpful to know because it can get discouraging with all the negative things that happen around us and to us. So, don't get distracted along the way. **Continue to believe and strive for the best because you were created by the BEST.**

Dressing My Inner Beauty

Tasheekia's Tidbits on How to Appreciate Yourself

- Be careful about comparing yourself to other people. Sometimes that can make you feel good or even inspire you to improve in some way. However, other times it can make you overlook what's truly good about yourself and cause you to feel bad.

- Think about times when you've done something good. Include those times when you've made a difference to somebody else by being helpful, kind, or thoughtful.

- Take part in activities that make you feel good, such as hobbies, reading, sports, or spending time with good friends.

- Don't be so afraid of failing that you are not willing to try something new. New experiences can help you grow and discover wonderful, new things about yourself.

- When you do fail at something, don't get down on yourself. Think about what you can learn from the experience and how you can do better next time.

- Think about things you do well. Take pride in your successes.

- Remember, the most important thing about us is what we are like inside, not what we own or what we've accomplished.

Scriptures to Think About

Steps to Being Your Best You

❧ Do not judge yourself against unrealistic or unreasonable expectations. Allow the Bible to be the standard that you use to measure yourself. The Bible is your guide to knowing God's expectations of you and learning more about Him. It has the answers to life.

> *"All Scripture is given by God and is useful for teaching, for showing people what is wrong in their lives, for correcting faults, and for teaching how to live right. Using the Scriptures, the person who serves God will be capable, having all that is needed to do every good work."*
>
> **– II Timothy 3:16-17**

❧ There is nothing wrong with feeling your best and doing your best. Set goals that will help challenge you to be your best, and set your heart to accomplish them no matter how long it takes.

> *"In all the work you are doing, work the best you can. Work as if you were doing it for the Lord, not for people."*
>
> **– Colossians 3:23**

Focus on being committed to more than your weaknesses. Celebrate your strengths and achievements, and understand God has gifted all of us to succeed in something.

"Remember that I commanded you to be strong and brave. Don't be afraid, because the Lord your God will be with you wherever you go."

– Joshua 1:9

Dressing My Inner Beauty Journal Page
How I Dressed My Inner Beauty Today

_____

_____

_____

_____

_____

_____

_____

_____

_____

_____

_____

_____

_____

_____

_____

_____

_____

Monday   Tuesday   Wednesday   Thursday   Friday   Saturday   Sunday

Dressing My Inner Beauty

Honoring My Value System is the Latest Fashion!

Your Value System

There are so many things that are important in life. Many people would probably go crazy if they had to live without something they thought was important. For instance, if your mom said that you had to choose between your iPod and PSP and could only have one, you would probably hit the roof. Why? Because these things have meaning to you. You use them daily, and they bring enjoyment to your life.

In order to figure out what things are really important in life, we have to honestly ask ourselves what we can't live without. One group of young girls was asked to list some things that they thought they could not live without. Immediately, they all listed things like "my pink boots", "my phone", "my social media", "my favorite shirt", or "my tablet". Without realizing it, all of the girls had listed items that would eventually break or go out of style as the things that they could not live without. It truly was an example of what they valued the most.

After giving them an opportunity to think about the things they had chosen, they were asked to make a new list and to really consider what was **important** in their lives. In a moment, one girl shouted out, "My soul is important." Another one said, "My family is important." Then the others began to catch on and shouted out similar things. Wow! Think about it. Could you live a meaningful life without church, friends, food, or education? I know that I could not!

If you have ever been to the beach, then you have seen what the waves of the ocean are like. Once a wave builds strength, it rolls forward and cannot be stopped. It's fun to swim out on a raft and try to catch the wave and ride it into shore. The same is true with your life. It is with great expectation that you will catch the wave of what's really important in life and ride like never before. Before getting on the wave, you must understand **values** and know that having a healthy value system will be **key** to living a successful life.

What is a **healthy value system**? Let's make it plain and simple. What you find important is considered what you find valuable. Knowing right from wrong, and choosing right over wrong, shows that you value what God values. For example, let's say that you have the opportunity to attend a sleepover with all of your friends. At the sleepover, you will have a chance to have facials, paint your nails, watch cool movies, and have long, fun talks with your friends. However, your grandparents, who live far away and whom you only see once a year, will be in town for one night ONLY on the very night of the sleepover. **What do you do?** Do you tell your grandparents, "Sorry, I already have plans," or do you tell your friends, "My grandparents are in town. It's important that I spend time with them, so I'll participate another time"?

I can see your faces now, LOL! Both things are important to you, but which is the most important? This is where the BIG **"P"** word comes into play. **"P"** stands for **PRIORITIES**. Yep, **PRIORITIES** is another word we will use to mean **IMPORTANT; RIGHT THING TO DO; YOUR MAIN CONCERN**. So, which did you choose? Most young people probably said that they wanted to have fun with their friends. A select few probably said, "Well, I can ask my friends to reschedule for next weekend, or I can just suck it up and miss out because I only see my grandparents once a year. I see my friends every day." It's all about putting **first** what needs to be **first**.

When figuring this "value thing" out, we must think about the things that are long lasting. When we focus more on the things that are lasting versus things that don't last, we can set **healthy priorities** which lead to **healthy value systems**. This is not to say that the fun things in life, such as shopping, watching TV, listening to music, and having fun with friends—things that often make you happy—are not of any value or can't bring some type of joy and fulfillment to your life. However, we need to prioritize these things so they are not placed before what really matters. You will have to make daily choices about what is important to you, and your top three choices are these:

- In order to determine what is important, you must decide whether or not your decisions line up with what God wants for you and what is in God's heart for you. You do this by reading and applying Biblical principles to your life.

- Ask if your decision will bring more value to your life.

- Ask if your decision will help someone else.

Now, you can go out and feed the homeless with your church or stay home and gossip with your BFF about the girl you can't stand in school. Let's consider feeding the homeless. God's word tells us to help those who can't help themselves. Therefore, we know this is in **God's heart** for us to do. **Does this bring value to your life?** Yes. Helping someone in need shows that you are caring, considerate of others, and selfless. **Will it help someone else?** Yes. You are helping someone feel better and you are helping your church make a difference in the lives of others.

Some people think that they will stand out more because of the people they hang out with, the clothes they wear, or how they look. You know how some of you sit up half the night trying to figure out what outfit you should wear to school that will look better than someone else's, and then spend the rest of the night texting or watching TV? Then, you get to school the next day only to remember that you had a test to study for, and that you are not prepared. **So what was important and what could have waited?** Nothing declares what's important to you more than your obedience to God, the way you treat others, and the respect you have for yourself. Regardless of what everybody else is doing, this is what will cause you to shine brighter than a diamond.

Since we are on the subject of value and what's important, I know sometimes you may feel overlooked, not needed, and simply not important to the people around you. One young person asked, "How can I be important when my mom would rather do drugs than take care of me? How can I be important when everyone I want to be friends with can't stand the ground I walk on? How can I be important when my dad wouldn't stay with my mom to raise me? How can I be important when nothing seems to go right for me, and I can't do anything well?"

Many things can make us feel like we are not important or that our life is a waste of time. It is so easy to look in the mirror and see yourself the way you think other people see you, but you are more than what you see in the mirror—you mean more than anything.

Hmmmm...so some may be asking, "I'm valuable even if I'm not the prettiest, best dressed, or smartest girl, or I don't live in a huge house?" Yep, you are! No matter how you look, or where you live, or who likes you or who doesn't like you, **God loves you**. Yes! God, the Creator of the world, loves YOU. As a matter of fact, He loves you so much that He did not think twice about whether or not to create you or whether or not to die for you. Yes, Jesus died for you knowing that you would make mistakes, knowing you would not be perfect, and knowing about your whole life before it even started. So not only should you have **values** and **prioritize** the important things in your life, but you need to know that you are most valuable to the heart of God, your family, and your friends.

Scriptures To Think About

Steps to Putting First Things First

- Before doing anything like choosing a friend, wearing an outfit, or deciding what you would like to be when you are older, determine its importance and base your decision on whether it pleases God. Be very careful not to label something as important because it is popular, fun, or just because you really like it.

  "Some people think they are doing right, but in the end it leads to death." – **Proverbs 14:12**

- Always remember that true treasure in life does not break or go out of style. The things that are of importance come from within you. These things called love, patience, self-control, peace, joy, forgiveness, and determination can only be seen in your actions toward yourself and toward others. They are long lasting.

  "Don't store up treasure for yourself here on earth where moths and rust will destroy them and thieves can break and steal them. But store your treasure in heaven where they cannot be destroyed by moths or rust and where thieves can break and steal them." – **Mathew 6:19-20**

❧ Know that you are important to God. When we receive Jesus as our Savior, He allows us to be a part of His royal family. He does not judge us like others. We are so valuable that God trusts us with His word to tell everybody about Him. When you accept who you are in Christ Jesus and understand it is He who brings this value to your life, everything in you and around you will begin to blossom.

*"But you are a chosen people, a royal priesthood, and a holy nation people for God's own possession. You were chosen to tell about the wonderful acts of God, who called you out of darkness into his wonderful light." – **II Peter 2:9***

❧ We have learned that everyone has valuable things that are precious to them. These things include church, family, education, friends, and, yes, even smart devices and favorite outfits. We have also learned about our value and how important we are, especially to God. We must also understand God's value and how He desires to be **first** above anything and everything in our lives. So, when we place Him first and consider how He feels about our choices, then our value system will reflect His.

*"Jesus answered the Pharisee, 'Love the Lord your God with all your heart, all your soul and all your mind'. This is the first and most important command." **Mathew 22:37-38***

Dressing My Inner Beauty Journal Page
How I Dressed My Inner Beauty Today

_____

_____

_____

_____

_____

_____

_____

_____

_____

_____

_____

_____

_____

_____

_____

_____

_____

_____

_____

_____

_____

_____

Monday   Tuesday   Wednesday   Thursday   Friday   Saturday   Sunday

Dressing My Inner Beauty
Modesty is the Latest Fashion!

Modest is Hottest

Growing up, I did not hear much about modesty. I am pretty sure it was required in many households, but I never heard the word because it was not brought up in conversation. As is the case with most young people, many of my cousins and I went along with every new trend or fad as it came out. One day when I was 12, I went to my grandma's house wearing hot pink lipstick. When I walked in the door, before she offered me any refreshments or snacks or even a "Hello", she offered me a look that could "kill"—a look that told me I had better get right into the bathroom and take off that lipstick!

Another day, I was leaving the house with some really short shorts on, and my brother yelled as loud as possible, "Mom! Look at your daughter. What does she have on?" And the look my mom gave me...well, let's just say I did not leave the house with those shorts on. It was hard to understand because everything I wore or seemed to be interested in was what I saw on TV, in videos, in my friends' closets, and what I thought at the time made me "fashionable". Just like most of you, I wanted to look good and feel good about myself.

I did not understand the importance of the words **RESPECT, VALUES,** and **MODESTY** until one day in the eighth grade my chorus teacher sat me down and talked to me. It was one of those teacher/mama talks. She started off with how beautiful and smart I was and how much of an influence I had on my peers. Then the "BUT" came in the next sentence, and the conversation took a quick turn. She had a mirror and told me to look at myself and imagine the future I was creating for myself if I did not change anything about my behavior, speech, or how I dressed. At that moment, I knew I was not being my best self, nor was I influencing others to follow in the right direction. She said that if I did not change, I would not have the success I dreamed of attaining.

My teacher continued to explain that there is nothing wrong with wanting to look good and keep up with the latest trends. Just think, if I did not conform in some way with the styles of the time, I would have still been wearing an afro and lots of polyester clothes from the 60's, and there I was in the 80's...Imagine that! She said that even with the latest fads and trends, I should still maintain a sense of **modesty**, because that is what being a young lady who demands respect represents. At that moment, I totally "**got it**"! I had bumps and challenges along the way, but I understood what she wanted me to see.

So, for those of you who had not heard of the word **modesty** before, and for those who think that if you become modest you will turn into this LAME, fashion-less girl who no one wants to be around, you need to understand that nothing could be further from the truth. The words of my chorus teacher from years ago are as true today as they were back then.

It is so important that you learn about modesty at the earliest age possible. Here is a definition for you: **modesty is the regard for decency of behavior, speech, and dress.** It all boils down to showing respect through the way you act, talk, and what you wear. Believe it or not, the word **modest** was very popular in the olden days. During that time, grandmothers, mothers, aunts, and even the community would teach and model the true meaning of modesty. In today's world, what our society portrays in the media and what we see from our peers often causes the idea of modesty to seem like it has the **YUCK** factor. Unfortunately, youth from all across the nation are drowning in deadly temptations that scream, **"Try me because I am fun, popular, and will make you cool!"** Sadly, in the world we live in, if you are not saying and doing what everyone else is saying and doing, and if you are not showing skin or doing what seems HOT, then you are NOT. At the same time, society is screaming for us to go along with the crowd, but it somehow forgets to scream out the dangerous and hurtful consequences that are a result of going along with the crowd.

Tweens and teens have always had a very difficult time transitioning because of the inward and outward changes going on with their body. It seems that at this age, young people are always trying to measure up, and therefore it can be a difficult time. Puberty and the pressure of fitting in are aspects that every young person has had to deal with since the beginning of time. A lot of the same pressures to do the wrong things have not changed. However, the difference today is that there are new ways and willing vessels by which to reach a mass amount of the youth at one time. Before television, radio, computers, cell phones, and video games, the temptation was limited. Most young people had to wait until they could hang out with their friends in the hallways at school or see them out in the neighborhood before they could talk about the latest news and happenings. Now, you can communicate with each other in an instant. You can text, email, or chat online about what's going on.

Due to of these new forms of communication, many parents now are allowing what parents years ago did not. Before the distraction of computers and cell phones, "dinner time" meant everyone would stop what they were doing, wash up, and sit down to eat a meal together as a family. Now, most moms are picking up pizza for one child and burgers for another while on the way home from work.

The negative influences of society have threatened to destroy the relationship that God intended families to have. As a result, many young people have made their parents the enemy because their parents have rules and guidelines that should be followed. The rebellion and disobedience of our youth is at an all-time high. Why? Well, this is in large part due to the fact that **modesty** has been neglected. Many young people want to look and act like what they see portrayed on TV and in social media. Think about this for a moment: **Matthew 7:16-17 relates**, "*You will know people by what they do.*" This means that the way you express yourself, behave, and dress speaks volumes about who you are and what you believe. As you strive to get closer to God, the ways you act, take care of yourself, and treat others will reflect your strengthening relationship with God. This does not mean that every day you will live perfectly.

Modest attire does not mean long dresses that hang down below your ankles, it means dressing with respect. Every young lady should invest in a full length/body mirror. You never know when you'll have to bend over or raise your hands, and you will want to be comfortable and prepared. So, before walking out of your home, you should do a quick "modesty" inspection, making sure your attire does not reveal parts of your body that should only be between you, God, and your future husband. If you are showing too much of your chest or belly with a spaghetti strap or crop top, add a cardigan or a t-shirt for a layered look and for coverage. For skirts that may appear too short, add tights or leggings for coverage. For fitted jeans or pants, add a longer, looser top for coverage. If your attire still looks too revealing after using these tips, maybe you should consider giving it away and getting a larger size.

You are God's representative on earth, and the way you carry yourself is important. You are an Ambassador for Jesus. There is a difference between a fan and a follower of Christ. However, you can strive to live according to God's standards, instead of "pop culture" standards. For example, your teacher represents the principal of the school. If your teacher comes to school wearing super short shorts, stiletto heels, and a bikini top, you will not take her seriously, nor will you take seriously the subject that she is teaching. Also, your mom would probably file a complaint with the school because your teacher is not following the appropriate dress code of a teacher. The same applies to you! When people see you and you are not showing respect in your speech, dress, or behavior, it is hard for them to believe that you are a follower of God. They will wonder what type of home you are being raised in and will question your morals. Remember, people are watching you and are ready to imitate you, so be that positive influence in their life.

Knowing what to wear is half the battle. Taking care of your body is the other half. The old phrase: "cleanliness is next to Godliness". Modesty and taking care of yourself go hand in hand. Bathing and brushing/flossing your teeth day and night are part of maintaining a healthy and clean appearance. Brushing your teeth, at least each morning and evening, helps to fight the bacteria left from food that could form under your gums and that causes gingivitis if your teeth are not properly cared for. Also, as you get older and enter puberty, your body begins to produce different hormones and chemicals that cause different reactions, such as sweating and body odor. Pay attention to certain smells. Odors come from the places we perspire the most, such as underarms or between our legs. Thankfully, we can often times smell ourselves before others can smell us, but to help with this, use **pH** balanced deodorants or powders.

Also, you can use panty liners as a great way to stay fresh, even if you have not started your menstrual cycle. For those emergency cases, it is a good idea to keep a little mini-purse or bag with lotion, fragrance, panty liners, and flushable wipes for use at any time.

Skin care is also important. Some of you may not be old enough to wear makeup, but remember there is nothing as wonderful as natural beauty. Keeping your skin healthy will limit the amount of makeup coverage you will need once you are old enough to consider wearing makeup. You can cover the majority of your body parts with clothing. However, the face is the hardest body part to cover. Therefore, it is the most sensitive body part because it is exposed to the sun and the elements all of the time. So make sure you are using a cleansing system based on your **skin type**. If you do not know your skin type, ask your parent or guardian to allow a professional skin care representative to take you through the steps of determining what is best for your skin. If you do not have problem skin or wear a lot of makeup, witch hazel acts as a great cleanser and toner, all for under $3.00 dollars.

To be sure you get the results you want, follow the basic steps to healthy skin.

1) First, use warm water with a facial cleanser, and massage in an upward motion on your face. This will open your pores. Allow the cleanser to soak through your skin, and then use cool water to rinse. This will close your pores, keeping your skin vibrant and soft. Remember, your neck is an

extension of your face, so cleanse your neck in the same way as you do your face for a more even and toned look. Stay away from fragrant soaps on your face. These types of soaps are known to irritate and dry out skin.

2) Your second step is to tone. (This step can be skipped for those who don't wear makeup.) Put a small amount of witch hazel on a cotton swab and rub it on your face in an upward motion. Don't forget your neck.

3) The last step is to use a moisturizer. You want to choose the right moisturizer for your skin type. Place a nickel-sized dot of moisturizer on clean hands and massage into your skin using a downward motion. Stay away from body lotions or fragrant lotions. As with soap, these can also cause irritation and dry skin.

Nail care is important, too! Imagine introducing yourself to someone and the first thing they see are ragged, dirty nails. YUCK! You do not have go to a nail salon to have healthy nails. Get your parents' permission first, and then make it a "girl's day" with you your mom, aunt, sister, or friends. While you may think the "loud" colors are popular, keep in mind that the louder the color, the more obvious the blemishes will be in the nail polish when it chips or begins to wear off.

Here are the basic steps to a mani/pedi (manicure/pedicure). First, you always want to remove any polish from your nails with polish remover. To do this, use cotton balls or cotton swabs and nail polish remover. Next, make sure you file or clip your nails to an even, appropriate length. Short, manicured nails look very sophisticated and chic. Soak nails in soapy, warm water for about 5 minutes. Clean under nails and pat your hands dry. Use hand lotion to moisturize hands, and then apply nail polish. This should be done once a week to keep a manicured look. Be aware of chipped polish and dirt under nails. You will notice that when you actually take time out and pamper yourself, you feel better about yourself.

Hair care is important for proper hygiene as well. Shampooing your hair according to your hair type will help to prevent split ends, breakage, and dry hair. When it comes to hair styles, remember, less is best. Find styles that fit your face and that will enhance your best features. Just because a hair style is trendy does not mean it always flatters your face.

Going to the beauty salon can be very costly. However, there are other options. Talk to your parents about going to a beauty school in your community. Beauty schools provide everything a salon would provide at a much cheaper cost. If you have a beautician, ask her to explain your hair type and how you can maintain your look at home. To save money, you can shampoo and style your hair at home, but always go to a professional licensed beautician for any chemical treatments.

Hopefully, you can now see how **modesty and taking care yourself go hand in hand**. Every young lady should know the difference between presenting herself **attractively** versus presenting herself **to attract**. When you present yourself to attract, you will often end up going overboard and attracting the wrong attention. However, when you present yourself attractively and modestly, you represent yourself and God in a positive light. Every FAB girl wants to look stylish and chic, and because you represent God as His royal princess, you should be stylish and chic. However, remember that your "Fabulosity" starts from within and then works its way out. In all you do to maintain a fabulous style, make sure **modesty** represents the total **you** in all you **are** and **do**.

Scriptures To Think About

Steps to Take to Live a FAB, yet Modest, Lifestyle

- Be a trailblazer for Jesus. At your young age, live a life for the Lord that will cause your friends, and even strangers, to desire the God you serve.

  "Don't let anyone look down on you because you are young, but set an example for the believer in speech, in life, in love, in faith and in purity." – **I Timothy 4:12**

  Here, God is telling you that when you live a life of modesty, you have the power to influence and cause people to change for the better.

- When you live a modest life, you have the power to save yourself and those you influence from trouble and even hell.

  "If you continue to live and teach **rightly,** *you will both save yourself and those who listen to you." –* **I Timothy 4:16**

- Do not live by the styles or standards of what you see on TV, read about in magazines, or hear about on the radio. This will take sacrifice on your part because it is tempting to want to be like or look like what seems popular. To sacrifice or let go of what you want in order to obey and please God says a lot about your love and commitment to HIM.

> *"So brothers and sisters, since God has shown us, I beg you to offer your lives as a living sacrifice to Him. Do not change yourselves to be like the people of this world, but be changed within by a new way of thinking." –* **Romans 12:1-2**

Your offering must be only for God and pleasing to Him, which is your spiritual service and worship.

- There is such power in our thought patterns. What we allow in our mind influences our actions. Keep in mind that your outward self—speech, behavior, and attire—reflects what you think. Keep your inner self pure with godly thoughts and you will be the queen of Modesty.

> *"Brothers and sisters, think on the things that are good and worthy of praise." –* **Philippians 4:8**

Think about things that are true and honorable and right and pure and beautiful and respected. If anything from the outer self does not line up with what you are supposed to be thinking on, then *stay away from it.*

🐷 Knowing who you are in Christ will keep you from allowing your outward beauty to define you and allow you to define your outward beauty by the beauty within you.

> *"A beautiful woman without good sense is like a gold ring in a pig's snout."* – **Proverbs 11:22**

Your outward beauty and style is just as useless as a gold ring in a pig's nose if you don't have respect, values, love, and faith.

Dressing My Inner Beauty Journal Page
How I Dressed My Inner Beauty Today

_____

_____

_____

_____

_____

_____

_____

_____

_____

_____

_____

_____

_____

_____

_____

_____

_____

_____

_____

Dressing My Inner Beauty
Being a Young Lady is the Latest Fashion!

Female by Birth; Lady by Choice

Have you ever heard the phrases, **"Act like a Young Lady"**, **"Sit like a Young Lady"**, or **"A Young Lady would not do that"**? We often hear a lot of things that we don't understand, and sometimes it is easy to take for granted the things being taught to us that will eventually make us better people. Well, all of this is not just talk. Being a young lady is a **big deal!**

Young Lady, you are a very special gift to the world. God did not make any mistakes when He created You. You know when you are writing and place an "I" where you should have placed a "T" and you have to erase your answer, or you accidently spill your beverage at the dinner table, or you bump into someone by mistake because you were not looking where you were going? Well, God is someone who has NEVER made a mistake. **God is perfect!** *God did not make any mistakes when he made you.*

I know that may seem strange because we all make mistakes and poor choices sometimes, but not God. He knows everything, sees everything, is the creator of all things, and can even be everywhere at the same time. WOW! He is the ultimate Super Hero. So, you have every right to shout out loud, "**I was created PERFECT and I am Proud!**" Yes, you were created perfect even if you look different or make not-so-perfect decisions.

I often hear young ladies say that they wonder why girls have to go through so much, when boys have it so easy. Well, it does seem like girls experience a lot—the puberty war, menstrual cycles, having to sit a certain way, and one day experiencing motherhood. I know sometimes it can seem like it is overwhelming to be a girl. BUT GUESS WHAT! Everything we go through is designed to push us into the perfect plans of God. Your gender may have come as a surprise to many people, but not to God. You were not born a female just to wear cute pink dresses and ponytails. **God had a very unique purpose in mind when He created you**.

When I was pregnant with my son, I found out that even before major organs are developed, the gender of the baby can be detected. This can happen as early as 10 weeks in the womb. At conception, a female begins to develop everything needed to one day become a mother. Our gender is not something we go to the grocery store and pick off of the shelf. Genetics play a major role in gender development, but God has ultimate control. By recognizing that the gender of a person is ultimately controlled by God, we can count it as a blessing to know that He must have a great purpose for our lives, and a special reason for creating us as females.

Much of society—music, politics, and TV—undermines the value of a female and the importance of treasuring whom God created us to be. Entertainers and singers often use extremely disrespectful lyrics to describe how they feel about females. Females themselves often act out of character and give a bad name to other young ladies who do respect themselves and take themselves seriously. This has caused many girls to battle with accepting their gender. Unfortunately, because of the negative influences around them, including pain, rejection, and even molestation, many girls desire to be the opposite of whom God created them to be.

Much of society has bought into the lie that it is okay to just be whom you want to be, but God will never change his mind about who He created you to be. In fact, it hurts Him to know that many girls do not look at themselves as a gift, but rather as a curse because they are girls. It is so important that you desire what God knows is best for you. He is such a gentleman! He will never ask you to do or accept anything that will harm you. When you desire God's will **first**, the thing that is pulling you out of His will, whatever it may be, will not be a temptation. You will pull away from it. The enemy seeks to deceive God's people and draw them into lifestyles that displease Him. You see, the enemy knows that it pains God to see one of His children go the wrong way. **You are complete, perfect, and just FABULOUS in Christ.** If you can realize this at a young age, you will not look to the world, friends, or "things of the world" to complete you.

The secret the enemy does not want you to know is that you can set your own trends and still be popular and influence many to come to the truth of who God is. The world was not created to complete you; you were created to complete the world.

So what does it mean to be identified as "just a female"? When identified as "just a female", you are limited to the basic things people can see to determine your gender. When God created Eve, the first female in the world, He created her with more than just good looks. He created her in His image—a righteous person, a helper to man, and the caretaker of the family unit. He did this so that generations of people would give glory to His name. Regardless of the scientific research or experiments you see and hear about, without male and female, this world could not create children, and this is one of the greatest things that God desires. He said it in His instructions to

Adam and Eve. He said for them to be **fruitful and multiply**. God's plan was for them to have children as husband and wife. So, your role as a female is more important than you think. Accepting that role, and walking proudly in it, just puts a great big smile on God's face!

Guess what? Your role does not stop at being a female. You have to do a little bit more to stand out. It is God's heart for you to understand how important this role is because in a world full of disobedience, peer pressure, and bad influence, you have to be more than just outwardly a female. **You have to be a Young Lady, a title given to a female who behaves properly and respectfully to both herself and to others.**

As you can see, there is a big difference between being a female and being a Young Lady. It is very common in today's world to see females in the crowd, but it really takes a lot to notice a young lady that does not go along with the crowd, respects herself, and desires to please God. We see females just about everywhere we go—at school, church, the mall, the movies, or just riding down the road. But how often can you point out a young lady dressing the part, speaking the part, and behaving the part?

God has given you everything you need to be a Young Lady. He has given you His word to guide and instruct you, His Spirit to strengthen you, boldness to encourage you, and a host of angels to assist you. You are well equipped to overcome any temptation the world may bring your way. You are worth so much more, and you have the opportunity to do so much more, when you walk in the role God designed for you. God started a good work in you before you were in your mother's womb. Let Him finish His good work in you so you can be a role model to other young girls who are looking up to you. YES! You may not be the most popular or smartest girl, but there are many girls observing your mannerism. Mannerism represents your behavior and demonstrates to others if you have manners or not.

What exactly are **Manners**? What may seem polite to you may seem rude to someone else. Each person is raised with different values and beliefs. Therefore, Manners mean a lot of different things to different people. For some, it is all about being nice. For others, it is about how you sit, or how you eat and act when dining. Some people do not understand why we have different manners for different occasions. For instance, we have dining manners, telephone manners, dancing manners, and manners when we are being introduced or introducing others. Almost everything we participate in has rules to follow in order to maintain an organized atmosphere and to keep us safe.

So how do we narrow it down? The **Golden Rule** is key to maintaining manners. **The Bible tells us to "treat others how we want to be treated."** If we can follow this basic rule in any occasion or situation we are involved in, we are sure to have appropriate behavior every time. As a young lady growing up, it is so important for you to know that behavior and the way we carry ourselves is not just for one gender. Everyone, girls AND boys, should behave according to the rules of proper etiquette and social settings. WHY? Well, put it this way—if we didn't behave using **Manners**, this world would be full of chaos and disruption.

I once thought that being a female was good enough to get me where I wanted to be in life, but I quickly found out that just being a female would not bring me respect, success, or appropriate attention. **God wanted more out of me**. Before coming to Christ, I was loaded down with many regrets, shame, and confusion about who I really was. But when I embraced the real "me" that He wanted me to be, my whole world changed. I only wish I would have done it at a much younger age.

So, the question is, "What is getting in your way of being the Young Lady God desires for you to be?" Think about the actions and desires that cause you to walk like, act like, and be like every other female. Make a goal to change those behaviors so that you can walk in the role of a FAB young lady. There are some things that seem okay and are not forbidden for you to be considered a young lady, but when you put these things that seem "good" before God, or misuse what is good, your Young Lady status could be in jeopardy.

Wisdom Nuggets Every Young Lady Should Know

Every Young Lady should know basic dining manners:

- Always watch the host, (the person that invited you).
- Place your napkin on your lap during meals.
- Place your napkin on your chair if you need to be excused and are not finished with your meal.
- Place your napkin next to your plate when you are done with your meal.
- Remember, every Young Lady has good posture at all times. Roll those shoulders forward, backward, and then drop. Make sure that your legs are closed and crossed at the ankle.
- Always start your meal after the host begins and everyone has been served.
- Always begin your meal by using the utensils from the outside to the inside.
- Dessert utensils will always be at the top of your dinner plate.
- Your drink will always be to your right.
- Your bread plate will always be to your left.
- Pass bread to the left as a courtesy.

- Remember to try it before you deny it, unless you are allergic.
- Use your inside voice to respect other guests.
- No cell phone usage at the table.
- Taste your food before you use seasonings.
- Always pass the salt with the pepper.
- Keep conversations clean and respectful.
- Never identify the server as "Hey You"! Find out the server's name at the beginning of dinner.
- Allow eye contact and use your hands to signal that you need assistance.
- Always chew with your mouth closed.
- Always chew quietly.
- Take small bites.
- No double dipping, (unless culturally the meals are shared).
- Do not express to others that your food is disgusting.

Scriptures to Think About

Steps to Maintain "Young Lady Status"

- It is easy to get caught up in the opinions of others and what is considered popular. You have to understand that as a Young Lady, what the world says you should be or do to gain acceptance does not overpower what God commands you to be and do. Your obedience to God will take you down the path of eternal success.

   "Obedience is better than sacrifice." – **I Samuel 15:22**

- It is easy to confuse the situations you are born into with who you are as an individual. You may not have been born into a perfect family, but you were created by a perfect God. And no matter what changes in life, His opinion of you will never change. You are His perfect work.

   "He is a Rock; His works are perfect and all His ways are just. A faithful God who does no wrong, upright and just is He."
   – **Deuteronomy 32:4**

- Many things have changed over the years. We have different fads, upgrades in technology, and even physical appearances. However, no matter how modern our society becomes or how we evolve, there are things that God intended to always be the same. He won't change His word or His love toward us.

   "I am the Lord, I change not." – **Malachi 3:6**

Date:_____

Dressing My Inner Beauty Journal Page
How I Dressed My Inner Beauty Today

_____

_____

_____

_____

_____

_____

_____

_____

_____

_____

_____

_____

_____

_____

_____

_____

_____

_____

_____

_____

Dressing My Inner Beauty
Healthy Friendships are the Latest Fashion!

Friendship Zone

Healthy friendships can bring the best out of an individual, just as unhealthy friendships can bring the worst out of an individual. When I was younger, I remember choosing a friend because we had the same sense of style. She liked spunky fashions mixed with crazy colors, and so did I. So, it was settled! She was my best friend, and no one could tell me differently. I learned the hard way that outward similarities would not produce a lasting friendship. My chosen best friend had mean tendencies. She shunned others and was very deceitful. I loved her outward style, but "her" inner style and "my" inner style did not coincide at all. I purposely drifted away and mingled more with people who had character traits and values similar to mine.

Friendships are vital and remarkable relationships. Healthy friendships allow you to get to know the person and create fun, memorable moments that last a lifetime.

The experience is great, whether you are learning together, crying together, laughing together, or growing together. Each experience, good or bad, is shared with someone that you love, trust, and enjoy being around. The friendship experience gives individuals the opportunity to become better and build stronger foundations as time goes on. Some people feel left out of the friendship experience because they don't have a lot of friends, or certain people are not their friend, or they have experienced friendships that did not last.

Well, well, well! **Let's have a Friendship Zone 101 lesson**. True friendships are not based on the number of people you connect with. True friendships are based on the quality of the people you connect with. An old saying I used to hear growing up was, "I'd rather have one person that I can call a true friend than many "frienemies" masking as friends." **Proverbs 18:14 says that some friends may ruin you, but a real friend will be more loyal than a brother.** People you have a great time with may not be great candidates for an authentic friendship. It is great to laugh and enjoy the company of others, however, a healthy friendship carries a lot more responsibility. True friendships share a strong bond based on similar characteristics and values. And guess what? A healthy friendship is a two-way street. You should never be in the friendship zone alone. Real friends work and sacrifice together, making the friendship strong. Beware of any friendship in which you are doing all the work. If you are the only one calling, giving, caring, and sharing, you just may be in the friendship zone alone. Distance yourself from anyone that claims to be your friend, yet pressures you or condones inappropriate behavior.

Report cards are out and you received a poor grade in math. A real friend would encourage you to do better, and if math is his/her favorite subject, he/she would offer to assist you. A "frienemy" would smirk, show you his/her "A", and never set up a study time.

Someone just embarrassed you in front of a popular group of peers. A real friend would help you keep your cool and talk you out of doing anything that you could regret later and that may tarnish your character. A "frienemy" would egg you on to behave inappropriately, and when you are asked to explain your actions, they will not be around.

You are wearing a FAB outfit and everyone is complimenting you. You are receiving extra attention, and your friend is not receiving any. A true friend will always be excited and happy to see you soar. Yes! A true friend will want you to soar and won't be intimidated when you do well. He/she will even join the crowd to cheer you on. "Frienemies" cringe when you are the star and they are not. They will become overly competitive and won't be satisfied until they "out do" you.

Real friends only compete to see who can be the Best Friend. When you start feeling uncomfortable, tense, and overwhelmed when trying to keep a friendship, remember, **you have Rights**. Yes, beautiful! You have **Friendship Rights**. Don't forget to exercise your Right to say "No!" You have the Right to set boundaries that no one should cross without your approval. Your most important Right is the Right to exit any relationship that is bringing you harm, negative pressure, or unrealistic expectations. Oops! I almost forgot to inform you that **your friend has these same Rights.**

Everyone enjoys being around people that they just "click" with. However, when it comes to real friendships, you want to "click" with the person who will not assist in **ruining** your future, but instead will add **productivity** to your future. A true friend doesn't find it cool or funny that his/ her friend is doing poorly in school or making poor choices by being disrespectful to his/her parents. A person that understands Real Friendship will understand the significance of valuing the same things. When a person does not value the important things in life, it is very difficult for him/her to value a true friendship when challenges and disappointments present themselves. It is very difficult to maintain a productive friendship that Jesus is not a part of. If a person does not value or embrace the act of kindness Jesus showed for us all on the cross, he/she will seldom know how to be a true friend or appreciate you as a friend. If a person is always on the receiving end and not willing to do the necessary work to maintain a friendship, then maybe it was not a friendship at all.

Through my life experiences—the ups and the downs—I have found no greater friendship than with the Lord Jesus Christ. **He is the ultimate friend**. In many relationships, we check for all the warning signs in people to see if the friendship is worth our time and effort, and when we find that a relationship is not worth our time or effort, we quickly move on to the next friendship zone. Jesus, being the ultimate friend, has already checked all the warning signs in us. He saw all of the wrong we would do, all of the people we would hurt, and even the times we would reject Him for other people that seem more fun. He saw all of this before we were born, and yet He gave His life so that **we** could have a chance at life. Jesus saw that without the shedding of His blood, His death, and His resurrection, we would not have a chance to be with Him for eternity. So, He took the ultimate chance and said, "I'll give my life for all that would believe in me. I will be their Savior, I will be their hope, and I will be their ultimate friend." **John 3:16 states that "God so** loved the world that he gave his only begotten Son so that whoever believes in him may not be lost but have an eternal life." God did this as an act of love for, and a sign of friendship to, all people who would receive and obey Christ as Lord. There are times that the one you call "friend" may not be available at the time you need a friend the most. Jesus promises to be with us at all times, and His presence is not limited to what you are going through, your decisions, or who is or is not there for you. You may feel unloved by others, or even left out within your family, but God is our ultimate friend. **Isn't it comforting to know that the creator of heaven and earth and all you see wants to be your friend?**

There were times in the Bible when Jesus felt all alone. One time He had to make a really big decision and needed his friends to stay up for one hour and pray with Him. When He came to check on them, He found them asleep. This was sad and disappointing for Jesus. He is the true meaning of having His friends' backs—He calmed the seas for them, made provisions for them, and taught them. These were the same friends that fell asleep on Him. This did not necessarily mean that they were not His friends. Jesus had to seek God for Himself in certain situations, and the Bible tells us that God sent angels to help Jesus. Jesus remained a faithful friend to the very ones who slept when He needed them most. Yet remember, **Jesus is the only Super Friend who can't make mistakes and is perfect in every way.** Unfortunately, we are not perfect, so we will need good friends to be patient and allow us room to grow. Most importantly, we will need our friends to give us second chances when necessary. As friends, it is important to learn together, grow together, and to become your "Best Selves" together.

Wait! Don't ditch your friend! There will be certain situations in which God will want you to lean totally on Him for help. Remember that everyone has a life, and problems and situations will occur that will cause even a real friend not to be available all the time. Keep your faith in Jesus and treasure true friends.

TaSheekia's Tidbits
Friendship Zone Checklist
Discussion

Check off the following statements to ensure you are connecting with Healthy Friendships. Journal how your friendships represent each.

- I can be myself without the fear of being judged.

- My friendship brings out my best attributes.

- I am not intimidated to share my friend with others.

- I can say "No" without the fear of my friend exiting the friendship zone.

- I do not feel pressured to impress my friend in order to be considered friends.

- I can set healthy boundaries, and a good friend will not cross them.

- I can trust my friend.

- My friend is loyal.

- There is shared giving in the Friendship Zone.

- My friend supports and encourages me to be and do my best.

- My friend tells me when I am wrong.

- I enjoy being around my friend.

- My friend gives me room to be silly and make mistakes.

- My friend listens to me.

- My friend and I participate in productive activities, i.e. Bible study, scrap-booking, studying, dance class, community service, and much more.

- My friend respects and honors the rules of my parents/guardians.

Scriptures to Think About

Steps to Maintaining a Healthy Friendship Zone

- Remember that your friendship can bring the best or worst out of a person. Do not base your friendship solely on laughs, similar fashion, and fun times. Be friendly to everyone, but be very careful as you enter the Friendship Zone.

  "Do not be fooled; Bad friends will ruin good habits."
  – I Corinthians 15:33

- The Golden Rule says it best. The friend that you are desiring to have is the friend you must be to yourself and to others.

  "Do to others what you want them to do to you." **– Matthew 7:12**

  This is the meaning of the Law of Moses and the teaching of the prophet.

- Be aware of the "frienemies" that hang out with you because of what you have to offer, your popularity, or because you are the fashionista. These types of friends can't embrace the best you because they want to be you. When you can no longer offer the luxuries they are looking for, many will exit the Friendship Zone. When you have nothing left to offer, your "so-called friends" will desert you and move on to the next person to use. The story of the prodigal son is a great example of this. Please read the example below and the full story in the book of Luke 15:32

"After he had spent everything, a time came when there was no food anywhere in the country, and the son was poor and hungry."

– Luke 15:14

Where were the friends he spent money on and had fun with?

When we connect to people that do not have the same value system as we do, there will always be confusion, the need to prove ourselves, and the pressure to fit in. If someone does not value the important things you value, you should reconsider stepping into the Friendship Zone. You may not agree on **everything**, but a productive friendship cannot exist unless you agree on the **important** things.

"Two people will not walk together unless they have agreed to do so."

– Amos 3:3

Date:_____

Dressing My Inner Beauty Journal Page
How I Dressed My Inner Beauty Today

_____

_____

_____

_____

_____

_____

_____

_____

_____

_____

_____

_____

_____

_____

_____

_____

_____

Monday   Tuesday   Wednesday   Thursday   Friday   Saturday   Sunday

Dressing My Inner Beauty
Using Your Voice is the Latest Fashion!

The Power of Your Voice

Young Ladies, your journey to confidence **without** compromise is approaching. Please bear with me a little longer. There are some more **great wisdom nuggets** I would like to share with you. The previous topics have assisted you in knowing who you are and feeling great about being you. The pointers about Values have opened your mind and eyes about the importance of having standards and drawing lines so that your character is not compromised. It feels good to know your worth, and this leads to positive choices and healthy relationships. I am excited as you draw nearer to **Celebrating the Beauty in Your Inner Beauty**! However, what is it to gain all of this insight and knowledge, yet have a fear of speaking out about it? You can have great qualities, strong friendships, a heart of gold, and no one will know because you have limited your influence by not using your voice. Most people are unheard not because people do not care, but because they have not utilized their most powerful weapon—**their voice**. It is time to speak out.

Your voice is **valuable** and **needed** for so many reasons. You can use your voice to build up or tear down, bring awareness, affirm yourself and others, and ultimately produce a positive mindset that will motivate you and others to walk in success. I am sure many people reading feel overlooked, ignored, and even useless sometimes. I reviewed *The Little Engine That Could*, and I was amazed at how the Little Engine used his words and the power of his voice to create a successful outcome when all of the odds were against him. His thoughts turned into words, his words turned into actions, and his actions produced victorious results. No matter what your situation looks like, thinking and speaking positively will give you the drive, motivation, and willpower to stay the course. *The Little Engine That Could* is an illustrated children's book that was first published in the 1930s by Platte. The story is mainly about being positive and optimistic in times of uncertainty and difficulty. A lot has changed since the publication of this book. Updated versions have been written, and even updated videos have been released. However, one thing that has not changed over the years is **the message** that the story conveyed. Difficult moments will continue to come, and we have to realize the power we have within ourselves and our words to carry on. The Little Engine was given a task that seemed too hard to complete. As he changed his mindset and used his words productively, he made it successfully to his destination.

I remember growing up in a single-parent home. My parents did their best with what they knew and what they had. I found myself complaining about what I did not have and how I wished I could live like some of my other friends that had both parents in the household with them. **The more negatively I talked, the worse I felt, and the more negative my choices became.**

One day, I met a girl living under worse conditions than I, yet no one could tell. She was always so sweet, positive, and successful in everything she did. One would have assumed that she had a great life. Well, we decided to talk, and she shared how her mother had passed away and that she was living with her dad and brothers. She also shared that her dad worked so hard and barely spent time with them, and she talked about how difficult it was to share things with him that she knew only her mom could have understood. She said, with tears in her eyes, that she would do anything to see her mom one last time. As tough as I tried to be, I began to tear up and asked, "How do you stay so positive, make good grades, build healthy friendships, and stay so active?" She stated that thinking, talking, and reacting negatively would result in negative outcomes. I immediately came back with, "But you do not have your mom!" And she replied, **"But I am still loved."** She was hopeful and allowed her positive words to create the peace and assurance she needed to keep her going towards her victory. This caused me to think about how my situation seemed so much worse because of how I used my voice.

Your voice matters! My friend's voice caused her to create a positive environment in a difficult situation, and this encouraged me to make conscious decisions to speak more positively. How are you using your voice? When you talk to others, do they leave with a positive or negative impression of you? When you are given an opportunity to make a difference, do you talk yourself into the task or out of it? Are you using your voice to influence someone to do something great or destructive? Think about these questions, then have a positive self-talk about how you are willing and determined to speak positively no matter how bad the situation may seem. There are so many young girls that are extremely positive, happy, and always using their words to encourage themselves and others. I personally give you five stars for your effort and willingness to speak positively. However, this is not the only scenario about our voice that can make a difference. Have you ever been in a situation where you needed to say how you felt, but did not want to cause harm, confusion, or drama? So, you just zipped your lips and did not say a word? Have you ever been in a situation where you were boiling mad and used too many words, and now you have many regrets? The way we communicate our thoughts and emotions can either lead us down a rocky road or create a smooth path. Our words are vital to our environment, relationships, and how people see us and ultimately treat us. When we take a positive and assertive approach, standing tall about a situation will reveal the confidence, assurance, and respect that we have for ourselves and for others. The young girl that zipped her lips may have to go through this situation again because she did not communicate her thoughts or express concern about how she was being treated. The girl that spoke hastily and rudely may have ruined a relationship, lost the respect of her peers, or damaged her self-image. It is hard to say how one will react in any given situation. However, when we form good habits of communication and positive thinking, we will more than likely set ourselves and others up for a positive outcome.

When you express yourself both verbally and nonverbally, there are **three communication styles** that will cause people to either be drawn to you or run away from you.

Assertive Communication is the art of standing up for yourself, others, or causes with confidence and respect for others.

Passive Communication reveals how shy, timid, and afraid you are.

Aggressive Communication is using one's influence in a negative manner.

Assertive Communication is the art of standing up for yourself, others, or causes with confidence and respect without undermining the value or rights of others and not ignoring your right to speak out. Communicating assertively reveals your respect thermometer for yourself as well as others, and your willingness to defuse drama. We spoke about maintaining a healthy self-esteem in the second topic. Well, **another newsflash!** Utilizing assertive communication will increase self-esteem and decrease stress. Let's take an assertive break and talk about the other two styles of communication for a moment.

Passive Communication reveals how shy, timid, and afraid you are. This attribute can often cause people to not take you seriously, overlook your concerns, and even take advantage of you. Listen, being quiet and cooperative is sometimes the wise way to respond, but when you shut down because of fear and intimidation, avoid conflict, go with what makes everyone else happy, or allow the voices around you to shape your desires, you become those voices and not yourself. Now, this confident you is really not you, but all of the words you've embraced from others. We want you to be you, **unapologetically.** Every time you hesitate to speak what's on your mind, you are apologizing for who you are! Every time you go along with something that goes against your values and that you really do not desire to do, you are communicating that you or your standards are **not** important at all. Now, I've been in passive situations before. Words from the experienced—it is more stressful not to speak out than to communicate to others how you really feel, even if they do not agree. This type of inner turmoil can cause you to feel nervous all of the time. **True story**! One time I was in a situation where it seemed as if everyone around me was better equipped for an assignment than I. The teacher began asking questions, and although I felt that I had the right answer, I did not say anything. At the end of class, my teacher asked why I allowed everyone else to share their opinions while I said nothing. I very nervously replied that I did not speak up because I did not want to be wrong, get picked on, or feel embarrassed. I felt sick to my stomach because I didn't get another opportunity, and left the class feeling as if I had let myself down. This type of ongoing stress causes self-resentment, resentment towards those who you should have stood up to, leads to unresolved anger, and is just not a healthy way to live. Passive communication causes you to not be the person that God intends for you to be. He wants us to be bold, compassionate, and passionate for Him. We are His vessels. He uses us to bring change, awareness, guidance, and even hope to those that may not know Him. Yes! **Your voice is used by God to draw people closer to Him.** You may be saying, "God does not need my voice! There are billions of people on earth! Why would He want to use me?" Let's take a Bible study break!

"Bible Break"

The Book of Esther is one of my favorite books in the Bible because it truly exemplifies the importance of assertive communication. I really would like for you to read the Book of Esther and then come back to this chapter. Go ahead, beauty! Ill wait… Ok. I trust that you read the entire Book of Esther and found that Esther was an orphan girl; she did not have her mother or father with her, and she was raised by her cousin, Mordecai. She was selected to be Queen to King Xerxes. As you read, Esther was a Jew, but had not disclosed her identity to the king because her cousin advised her not to. The king promoted one of his workers, Hamon, with a seal of honor higher than all of the other nobles, and all of the royal officials had to bow to him at the gate. Well, Mordecai refused to, and this angered Hamon. Hamon went to the king and set a plot to destroy an entire lineage of Jews.

The king favored Hamon, and agreed to sign a decree that commanded all the Jews be killed. He placed his signet ring on the decree{a promise that could not be broken}. When Mordecai heard of the decree to kill the Jews, he was so upset that he ripped off all of his clothes and cried out loud. He was able to pull it together and get a message delivered to Esther. He asked her to go before the king and request favor for the Jews. Oh boy! Esther was afraid and sent a message back to Mordecai relating that if she went before the king without being called, she could be killed. She didn't want to risk her life because she was quite comfortable being pampered, held at high regard, and not saying one word about who she was or of her family. Mordecai sent a message back stating that she must not forget that she was still a Jew, and if the king found out, she would not escape. He said to her that perhaps she was assigned the Queen's position for such a time as this, and it was time to speak out. She was still nervous and hesitant, but asked for everyone to pray and fast with her for three days. After the prayer and fasting, she went before the king and would face whatever consequences came her way. God gave Esther favor. She was able to share her concern for her people, and the king reversed the decree.

There was a leader inside of Esther and there is a leader inside of you. What haven't you spoken out about?

What do you say when someone is being teased or talked about? Are you ashamed or afraid that if you speak about your love for God, you'll being called lame or be rejected by your peers? Your voice just may cause someone else to admit their love or need for God. Remember, when people are passive, they can't lead productively. They are normally passed by, overlooked, and not taken seriously. What about the girl that spoke hastily and rudely, and now has regrets? She is not off the hook. Her communication style would be considered aggressive.

Aggressive Communication is using one's influence in a negative manner. Aggressive communication intimidates, overpowers, and is expressed in an inappropriate manner. Most aggressive people feel that they are OK because they are "keeping it real" or "telling it like it is". A student of mine stayed after class one day and ask why her peers avoided being around her. She felt that she was not being fake or phony and carried the attitude that screamed, "I can't help it; I say what's on my mind!" I had to explain to her that I was very proud that she did not back down or let others walk over her, but I added that she needed balance. She needed to understand that screaming, threatening, or fighting in the heat of the moment will not resolve conflict; it will magnify it. I shared that most of her peers felt she was bossy and did not care about the needs or opinions of others. She began to look sad because no one had ever told her that this type of communication would sometimes get you what you want, but with the high price of losing friends and opportunities, and accumulating many regrets. As I explained the difference between **assertive** and **aggressive**, she agreed that she could still say "No" or share her views and feelings without humiliating, disrespecting, or undermining her peers. She could stand up for herself, others, and what she believed in with a stern, yet respectful, attitude. Self-expression is very important because we all want to be heard. Assertive communication allows others to hear you and respect your stance. **The leaders that are worth following use their voice not to intimidate, but to motivate, educate, and inspire positive change wherever they are!**

TaSheekia's Tidbits

Assertive Checklist

- I will use my words in a way that builds and not tears down.
- I will stand up and speak out without fear or intimidation.
- I will not allow the negative words of others to define me.
- I will use my words to communicate effectively and productively with others.
- I will use my words to share Christ with others.
- I will use my words to create a positive attitude in difficult situations.
- My words have power, and I choose to use my words to inspire, motivate, and enrich the lives of others.
- I will be careful of the words I embrace and the advice I take.
- I will be assertive with people and aggressive with my ambitions.
- I will speak out on causes and matters that are dear to my heart. I will be heard!

Scriptures To Think About

Steps to Maintaining an Assertive Voice While Standing Tall

- Remember that our words have the Power of Life or Death. You can fuel or defuse a negative situation by what you say. You can also encourage yourself and others to see the bright side of any situation with your words.

  "The tongue has the power of life and death, and those that love it will eat its fruit." – **Proverbs 18:21**

- My grandmother used to say, "You can draw more bees with honey than vinegar." She was encouraging me to speak out, but never undermine, tear down, or insult anyone. In life, we have the ability to either build or burn relational bridges with our words. We never know who we will need at any given time! So, it is imperative that we deal with people as if we may need them tomorrow.

  "Let your conversation be gracious and attractive so that you will have the right response for everyone." – **Colossians 4:6**

❧ Many situations cause us to be clouded with our emotions, and many people either zip their lips and harbor bitterness or let it all out and have regrets. It is very important that we communicate in love and diffuse issues with people as peacefully as possible. When we are standing up for a cause for ourselves, we need to communicate and react the way the Bible instructs us to. When we apply biblical principles to our conversations, we get our point across and show the light of God at the same time. It is a Win-Win Situation.

> *"Be angry without sinning. Don't go to bed angry."*
> *– Ephesians 4:26*

❧ One of the greatest ways we can use our voice is being a witness for Christ. He needs bold, compassionate, and knowledgeable people of His word to spread the gospel everywhere. Jesus even encouraged those who followed Him not to keep the gospel for themselves. It is good news, and we are encouraged to live it and share it. What a great cause to speak about and share with others.

> *"So wherever you go in this world, tell everyone the good news."*
> *– Mark 16:15 (God's Word Translation)*

☙ Your words are what God awaits. He loves for us to communicate with Him, ask for guidance, and even tell Him when we have messed up and need forgiveness. He is always listening and ready to forgive us, assist us, and speak back to us.

"The Lord remains near to all who call out to him, to everyone who calls out to him sincerely. He fulfills the desire of those who fear him, hearing their cry and saving them."

– Psalm 145: 18-19 (International Standard Version)

☙ The greatest words I've ever proclaimed changed my life forever. If I understood the depths of my words at your age, I would have taken advantage of this opportunity sooner. I thank God for his patience, unconditional love, and opportunity to receive Him as my Lord and Savior. I believed (respected God) and I confessed (spoke), and at that moment, God saved my soul and I began my journey as a Christian. You have that same opportunity. I was not in church or with a group of people when I realized who God was, the importance of honoring Him, and that tomorrow may not be available for me to receive the best gift ever-Salvation. I was on the phone with my friend's sister and she prayed with me and then challenged me to give my whole heart to God, follow Him, and not look back.

"If you confess with your mouth that Jesus is Lord and believe in your heart that God raised him from the dead, you will be saved."

– Romans 10:9 (NLT)

"If you use your mouth to say, 'Jesus is Lord,' and if you believe in your heart that God raised Jesus from the dead, you will be saved."

– Romans 10:9

Side Note: If you repeated this scripture and desire to accept Jesus Christ as your Lord, please ask your facilitator for church recommendations, or see your youth pastor or pastor for more information about this amazing journey!

Dressing My Inner Beauty Journal Page
How I Dressed My Inner Beauty Today

_____

_____

_____

_____

_____

_____

_____

_____

_____

_____

_____

_____

_____

_____

_____

_____

_____

_____

_____

Dressing My Inner Beauty

Talking About I.T. is the Latest Fashion!

Let's Talk About I.T.

*L*et's Talk About I.T. is dedicated to my "Thinker" Girls. I.T. stands for Internal Thoughts! Many times, we attempt to figure things out internally. It is so important that we verbally seek help and guidance. The world is moving at a fast pace. Many things are changing, new laws are being implemented, and what was forbidden 10 years ago has been embraced as a new way of living. Never accept or embrace anything based on the popular belief system. Always seek advice from a trusted adult. I hear you asking, "Why can't I ask my Friends?" Friends are great for venting, sharing great experiences, and bonding, but not necessarily for answering life's questions. My grandmother used to call friendship guidance "the blind leading the blind". When you allow trusted adults to advise you, you have a better chance to get an experienced answer.

Many laws and bills have been passed, and behaviors and images promoted throughout media may not coincide with your **Value System**. Going along with what's popular is out of style. Your life, future, and image are being jeopardized every time you make a decision with uncertainty. Ask! **Asking is our new policy.** It is so important that before you go along with any idea, you do your own research, ask questions, and fully understand what you are embracing. Many girls are very hurt, confused, and stressed because they are missing answers! **So, we are going to Talk About I.T.**

Over the past 12 years, I have facilitated programs, mentored girls, and preached at many worship centers. I've always included a time for girls to ask questions anonymously. Many girls are shy, afraid, or just don't think it's important to talk about the things that affect them. I have pulled many questions from my Talk About I.T. Box and I want to share some of those questions and answers with you. I hope you receive the necessary guidance you need, and the motivation to ask questions that are dear to your heart.

I am grateful to know so many influential women who care about your future. These questions below are answered by professional, intelligent women who believe that no question is too dumb. We also have a gentleman that assisted with a Beauty question. The answers to these questions are not to diagnose or solve all of your problems. We want to assist you on your journey to **Becoming the Best You.** Please consult with the appropriate people before making any decisions. So, here we go! Let the questions begin! We are now about to enter the Internal Thoughts of Girls Today. Your only assignment is to ask questions.

Scriptures To Think About

Steps to Maintaining the Confidence to Ask

🐭 Many people mislead others, remain confused, or destroy themselves because they do not ask questions, educate themselves, or listen to sound advice.

> *"My people are destroyed from a lack of knowledge"* – **Hosea 4:6**

🐭 It is very important that we seek advice from those who are trusted and wise. Never shun or ignore someone that can lead you on the right path.

> *"Plans go wrong for lack of advice; but with many advisors they succeed"* – **Proverbs 15:22**

🐭 It is ok that you don't know everything. It is **not** ok not to ask. The Bible is filled with answers to all of life's issues. Be very careful when receiving advice. No advice is good if it is not approved by God.

> *"If any of you lacks wisdom, you should ask God, who gives generously to all without finding fault, and it will be given to you"* – **James 1:5**

Let's Talk About I.T.

Questions & Answers

Q.   What are the benefits of writing in a daily journal? How can writing my feelings make a difference in my life? **(Reflection)**

A.   I've always been a big thinker and critical analyzer. Sometimes, I didn't feel confident that those around would understand or hear me without judging me. When I began to journal, my entries were affectionately called my "Dear God" letters. Journaling has always helped me to express myself freely and to reflect back on past times to see answers to prayers and promises from God. My journals are my keepsakes.

The above answer was submitted by Monshay Gibbs.

Q.   I hear so many people talking about political issues, and I've learned a lot about government in school. How important is political involvement? What ways can I be politically active at a young age, and what are some appropriate groups I can join? **(Politics)**

A.   Young people are in training to take over the world when the older generation passes away. Political involvement is very important because politics is an important human activity, and young people should learn about it so they can play their part well when the time comes. Young people can participate in school board meetings where they can learn about the different issues and struggles, and express concerns and opinions on ways to improve their learning environment. One of the ideas I would propose is for a young person to start a teenage political club at their school with the mission and purpose being to find ways to improve their quality education in the current school they are attending. Therefore, the young are encouraged to study political works, observe the way political parties function, and vote as soon as they come of voting age.

The above answer was submitted by Beatrice Jacquet, President for the Haitian-American Democratic Club of Lee County

Q.   What advice can you give me about blended families? My parents are not together anymore, and each is dating other people. I love both of my parents and I don't want to seem disloyal by accepting their respective mates. **(Family)**

A.   This is a difficult transition for any young person or adult. You must realize that both of your parents love you and you are not the cause of them not being together. However, both of your parents deserve to be happy. Accepting their mates is not being disloyal to your parents. Having more parents sometimes can be beneficial.

The above answer was submitted by Beatrice Jacquet, President of the Haitian-American Democratic Club of Lee County

Q.   I feel so left out because my mom is not a part of my life. What are some ways I can cope with this? **(Family)**

A.   As a woman who lost her mother at the tender age of 14 years old, I totally understand how it feels not to have a mother in your life. There are a few things that I would suggest:

- 👑 For whatever reason she is not a part of your life, make it your business to forgive her and don't hold on to bitterness or anger. People do what they *think* works best for them, not necessarily what is right. Understand that it is NOT your fault and love her for *who* she is, not *what* she has or has not done.

- 👑 Get an adult mentor that you trust, respect, and admire. One of my favorite scriptures says that there is safety in a multitude of counsel. (Proverbs 11:14) That means that when you have wise, mature adults who serve as guidance, you can avoid many pitfalls and even get ahead in life, no matter your situation or circumstance.

✦ Take what you're feeling and help others. Our hardships in life are meant to make us stronger, and even more importantly, they help to uplift, encourage, and inspire others who may be dealing with similar issues. Be gracious by sharing your life story to help improve someone else.

The above answer was submitted by Achie McEachern, Life Coach/Speaker/Youth Advocate, Unusually Remarkable Life Solutions, LLC.

Q. I have been looking for ways to show my parents how much I appreciate them. I do not have money to buy gifts. What are some other ways I can show my gratitude? **(Family)**

A. *"Wherefore comfort yourselves together, and edify one another, even as also ye do."* **1 Thessalonians 5:11 (KJV)**

Words of Encouragement:

Taking the time to show your parents you appreciate them does not require a monetary investment. To start, take advantage of the moments that you are alone together to let Mom or Dad know that you love them and appreciate them. As a teen, you have grown and become aware of when a parent may be facing some kind of adversity or issue. Parents need encouragement just as young people do. I remember once when my then-16-year-old daughter encouraged me through one of those times. It is fifteen years later, and I still remember what she said and how her words impacted me and put wind in my sails at that very moment. Her words were, "Mom, you are very special to me and very special to God. He gave you all of this to bare because He trusts you and has faith in you that you have what it takes to handle this...I love you."

Have Fun:

Take time to just have fun with your parents. Make a Mommy-me- date or Daddy –me-date. So you could say, "Mom, let's order $5 pizza or Chinese food and rent a $1 movie (then it was $1), just me and you." Can I tell you those were some of the best Friday nights I ever had? Or, "Dad, let's go fishing or let's go to the park and play tennis, ride a bike together, go swimming, or go roller skating."

Creative Artistic Crafts or Projects:

My children were very creative because their parents were involved in the arts; dancer (mom) and musician/artist (dad).

Skits, music and dance concerts:

The most fun times were the mini, full-scale productions with music. Drama, dance, costumes, lights, and curtains were all created with objects found around the house. We are talking bed sheets for curtains, flashlights for spotlights, and mommy and daddy's clothes from the closet. We reenacted skits from Saturday Live, Night Fever, Fame, Sarafina, and Dr. Martin Luther King. This used to happen regularly before the Non-profit Colours School of the Arts was even thought of!

A gigantic 4x3 collage of fun family times carefully put together from many pictures uniquely cut and arranged and framed is something that I will always keep and always puts a smile on my face when I look at it! This was done almost 20 years ago!

Make love notes and handmade cards that express how you feel about your parent. I have a very thick file of cards and notes. I call it my "Love Jones" file. LOL!!! But the love notes are from all my children! Some of the notes were very strategically placed and were poems, words of encouragement, love, and affirmation. Some were just very funny jokes that caused me to laugh when I really needed to laugh more than anything else. Laughter is good medicine for the soul. Sometimes, along with the love notes, came a little bouquet of wild flowers picked from around the yard.

Create an art piece out of clay or wood from your art class that specifically conveys, "I was thinking of you when I made this sculpture/painting/piece of furniture."

Pamper Them:

Parents, single moms especially, will tend to forget to pamper themselves. Therefore, foot massages, pedicures, manicures, back massages, back scratches, bubble baths, and home-made facial masks are all thoughtful gifts.

Feed Them:

Breakfast in Bed or a full, four-course meal (if you can cook) on any given day will be appreciated. You can do this even if it isn't Mother's Day or Father's Day!

Clean the House:

It was always the strangest, yet the best feeling ever to walk into the house when it was cleaned from top to bottom and a favorite meal was already cooked. Do what is expected of you (your chores), and go beyond. This really spoke volumes to me as a hard-working, single mom!

The above answer was submitted by Sharon Hill, CEO & Founder of Rhema Consulting and Author of Born to Lead, "Awaken Your Purpose".

Q. I deal with a lot and feel overwhelmed most of the time. My parents feel that I have no worries because I do not have adult responsibilities. How can I cope when my parents think I am fine? **(Family)**

A. As I read this question, I am reminded of the struggles that our young people face. Your parents are not going to understand what you are going through all of the time, and this is why I believe that every young person needs to have a relationship with God. Why? Because He always understands what you are going through, and He knows how to help you. The best way to cope when your parents think you are fine, when in actuality you need support, is by calling on your Heavenly Father. When you call on Him, He will send the support you need. Being in a relationship with Him makes this process more effective.

One important thing to note is do not judge or resent your parents for not recognizing where you are, how you are feeling, and how much you are handling, but see them as humans. Recognize their limitations and allow their limitations to open your eyes to the need for:

- A relationship with someone who knows you better than yourself.
- A relationship with someone who understands everything that you feel.
- A relationship with someone who is able to guide you through all things.

"Before I formed thee in the belly I knew thee; and before thou camest forth out of the womb I sanctified thee, *and* I ordained thee a prophet unto the nations." **Jeremiah 1:5** (The key here is to recognize that God knows you first and best.)

"For we have not "an" high priest which cannot be touched with the feeling of our infirmities; but was in all points tempted as *we are, yet* without sin. Let us therefore come boldly unto the throne of grace, that we may obtain mercy, and find grace to help in time of need." **Hebrews 4:15** (He understands all you feel and wants to send help.)

It is also good to talk to a trusted adult, one who you can say without a doubt has godly wisdom and has the lifestyle to match their talk. God sends us people to guide us in life, and they come in the forms of friends, pastors, relatives, and so on. Tap into them if you can. The goal is to get help and not to try to cope alone.

I remember when I was about 15 years old, I was in a similar position. The only difference was that it was my teachers and not my parents. You see, I was blessed with being able to grasp things in class very well, so oftentimes when I did not understand something, my teachers did not believe me. Other students would get a lot more support because my teachers thought that I was fine. I prayed about it first, and then I spoke to other authorities and got help.

Another way to cope is by taking your eyes off of your problems and focus them on others. Doing this somehow has a way of healing you and giving you what you desire. Therefore, from a place of the very under-standing that you seek, take the time to pray for your parents as they, too, have a lot of responsibilities and sometimes feel like no one understands. Ask God to give them the wisdom they need to guide you. Find someone who feels misunderstood and be there for that person.

At the end of the day, this is what you should un-derstand—you are the child of your mother and father, but you belong to God. He created you and He knows what's best for you, even when your parents do not know. A relationship with Him is the most important relation-ship you will ever build in life. He is all knowing and all powerful; who better to have a connection with? God is the best source to help you cope, not only when your par-ents do not understand, but when everyone else and even you do not understand. So give what you desire, seek godly council, and build your relationship with God.

I encourage you to stay strong as you are not alone, and many have gone through what you are going through and have come out strong. Understand that what you are going through is often experienced in life by many, even your parents.

The above answer was submitted by Tanya Price, Family Life Expert, Famti (Family Training Institute.)

Q. My Father is absent, and sometimes I look for love and attention in boys and end up making poor choices. What is the best way to deal with day-to-day life without the presence of my Father? **(Family)**

A. Beloved, the first thing you need to know is that your father not being in your life has absolutely nothing to do with you. You are a rare and precious jewel who is loved more than you can possibly imagine by your Father in Heaven. Seeking love and attention from the opposite sex is not going to fill that void that you are feeling. What it will do is cause you to get into situations or make decisions that you are not ready for and receive unwanted attention. It will also cause people to form opinions of you that are not a true reflection of who you really are. Here are some things that I found helpful while growing up without a Father:

- Learning about God, how much He loves me, and what He desires for my life. Jeremiah 29:11 and Luke 12:7 are great verses to reference.

- Focusing on the things that I really liked about myself and building my self-esteem and confidence.

- Finding a mentor or group of mentors that I could trust to confide in but to also guide me on life choices.

- Get a journal and write out your feelings. It helps to let things out.

- Connect with other young ladies that you can trust that may be in the same situation and can relate to what you are going through. Ladies who care about you and want to see the best for you.

Please keep an open heart and an open mind when it comes to your father and try to forgive his absence. Not for him, but for you and your happiness.

The above answer was submitted by Alicia Graham, Managing Partner, Pro Player Insurance Group.

Q.   I love hanging out with my friends, but my parents make me feel bad for not spending more time with my family. **(Family)**

A.   Being around family is vital. Although your friends appear to be trendier and have more in common with you, your friends can not effectively explain to you the things you experience and go through. Friends your age can only give limited advice. They are looking for answers just like you. On the other hand, family members have already been where you are now, and believe it or not, teen you has more in common with your family than you realize.

Think about it, being around family is like looking in the mirror. You identify with your family, such as my hair is long like... I am short like... I talk just like... I am out-going like... Being around family teaches you about you.

The above answer was submitted by Feleycha Watson.

Q.   I am currently in a foster home. Every day I am here, I hate my parents more. How can I cope with not having my own family? **(Family)**

A.   Remember, no one can take the place of your own family. Think of your foster home parents as extra indi-viduals placed in your life to help you become an amazing person. If you don't give them a chance, you may miss out on opportunities to grow, become stronger, and have new experiences to share with your peers. Think of foster care as a platform for you to reach other foster youth who you can relate to. Think of foster care as a place for you to teach your foster parents what you as their foster child needs. Foster parents have no manual to be foster parents. This is your chance to let them know the do's and the do not's when it comes to having a child in their home who just wants to belong and be loved. Lastly, remember, your biological parents and family CANNOT BE REPLACED!

The above answer was provided by
Nicole Marchman, MSW, Foster Alumni Founder & CEO of
None Lost Movement.

Q. What are some ways I can invest and budget at a young age? **(Money)**

A. Anytime you receive wages, a monetary gift, etc., decide on a portion to always set aside in a separate savings account or place where you can see it grow. For example, always put 5-10% into savings. If you do not need money for necessary expenses, put more away. Budget for savings just as you would for other items. Set a goal for necessary items and a goal for a savings amount that you would only touch in case of Emergency. It's a Mindset!

Q. Why are these habits important to start? (Money)

A. This is one of the most important habits that you can create for yourself to last for the rest of your life, and to assure yourself of a more secure future.

Life is full of challenges, many of which will be out of your control. Being without reserve funds could make you powerless to control the direction of your life.

Use your money wisely. Ask yourself, how badly I need another pair of shoes, a new lip stick, etc...

Always having some reserve funds (Savings) will give you control and options in your life.

The above answer was submitted by Martha F. Nagata of the Zonta Club of Ft. Myers.

Q. I need help with my prayer life. What are the basic steps to prayer? **(Relationship with God)**

A. Some young people shy away from prayer because it seems awkward to talk to someone they do not see. We can't see the wind but we know it's there when we feel its cool breeze. It's the same with God! All we have to do is look at creation and know that man did not create it and it did not create itself. Prayer is simply a Conversation with God. It is very important to talk to God for direction and to strengthen our relationship with Him. Imagine having a great friend that you never talk to. Now, that's awkward. God is more than a friend, He is our creator. He loves to hear from us.

Here are some great tips that will assist you on your Prayer Journey:

- Prayer is a beseeching of God. Beseeching is a prayer of pleading. Have you ever wanted something so bad that you could feel it, taste it, and even smell it?

- Prayer is frequently commanded of us in the Bible. Our prayers must be sincere. Our prayers must be offered in faith. We must believe that God is the one who hears and the one who answers.

- The Lord's Prayer in Matthew 6:9-13 is a great model prayer. This prayer covers a lot and will get you off to a great start.

- Don't feel like you have to pray the same way every time. There are different kinds of prayers:
  - ✟ Secret Prayer - When you create a place in your room or home and talk to God alone.
  - ✟ Social Prayer - A public prayer in the sanctuary or church when we pray with others about various matters.
  - ✟ Intercessory Prayer – Is commanded. This is the prayer that causes us to put our needs and desires aside and pray for the needs of others.

The above answer submitted by Prophetess April V. Washington.

Q. Since no one is perfect, why is purity so important? How can I obtain a pure life overall? **(Relationship with God)**

A. I wouldn't equate perfect with purity. According to Webster's Dictionary, Perfect is something completely free from fault or defects/lack. When I first read the word Purity and/or Pure my thoughts were innocence, without alteration, respect, and clean. Being pure or having purity is a gift, it's how you live your life, it's having character, and it's attainable. Purity is so important because it's key to building your character, your self-worth, and your confidence to do the right thing when no one is watching. This is what we call integrity. You are your own personal story, and you build your storylines that can take you down paths that will build you or paths that will set you back. Build a story of your life that a stranger could read and become encouraged in knowing that they, too, can overcome obstacles in being a better, stronger individual. Your life is your testimony of the things God can and will do. You obtain a Pure life by reading and adopting what God says about you. The Word of God is our road map through life. The BIBLE is: Biblical Instructions Before Leaving Earth. If you never read the Word, you will not have instructions on life and will walk around aimless, without directions. Proverbs 30:5 speaks of God being pure and He will be a shield for those that take refuge in Him. Matthew 5:8 tells us Blessed are the pure in heart, for they will see God. Just those two scriptures should give you confidence in knowing that while here on earth in your pureness of heart, God will be your shield through your everyday walk that will award you in the end to see Him again. Living a pure life is loving God so much that you refuse to find yourself guilty, altered, unclean, and disrespected. Being perfect is unattainable whereas having a pure life is something we all have the ability to obtain.

The above answer was submitted by Minister C. Lynn Thomas, Author/Motivational Speaker and Founder Fill My Cup Book Mobile

Q. What advice would you give someone that is being bullied, or to the bully him/herself? **(Bullying)**

A. First, for the person being bullied, it is important to know that nothing is wrong with you. Oftentimes, people bully because they see in you something that is lacking in them. Do not think that you are not enough. You are more than enough. You deserve to be treated with respect, so it is important not to keep silent. Tell your family, the school, or someone that you trust. Keeping silent tells the bully that it is ok when it is not ok. It won't go away with silence. It's like putting a band-aid on an oozing wound. The band-aid can't hold the wound.

For the person that is the bully, I would ask what happened. Why would you feel the need to cause someone harm? Don't you know that you are harming yourself and your own dignity? I would tell them that they are more than enough. I know that you are acting out because you need to be seen or heard. You do not need to hide behind walls of anger, hurts, and pain. Healing comes when we face it, when we bring it to light. Bullies need love and healing, and hurting someone else is not the answer. It only leads to a destructive life. Please speak to someone that you can trust and that can help you deal with the deep- rooted hurts and pain. Speaking to someone can bring about healing and a change in behavior.

The above answer was submitted by Yemisi Oloruntola-Coates, Manager, Diversity & Language Services.

Q.   What is so important about going to college? No one in my family attended college and they all seem to be doing fine. **(College/Post-Secondary Education)**

A.   I want to start by explaining that post-secondary education consists of more than college. While I am an advocate for college education, I realize that college is not a necessary route for everyone to achieve their life's purpose. Education after high school may include junior college, university, trade school (i.e. plumbing, cosmetology), or obtaining various credentials through licensure/certification.

Post-secondary education is important for many reasons. First, it gives you the necessary foundation to embark on whatever profession or entrepreneurial endeavor you have decided to pursue. Most careers require that you have some level of education before you can enter the workforce in that area. The educational path required will give you that basic level of education or training required.

Secondly, it can expose you to experiences and people you otherwise would not have had the opportunity to interact with. When I went to college, I gained lifelong mentors, contacts, and friends that became resources for me once I entered my profession. Many of those connections helped to give me job opportunities that I did not necessarily qualify for. I've also been able to help some of those people.

Next, it challenges you to achieve and go further than you've probably ever pushed yourself. Prior to college, I never had to study for tests and, therefore, I had not developed any type of study skills. Things that usually came easy to me became a challenge. I had to rely on my faith and develop a work ethic if I wanted to accomplish what I had set out to do. Ultimately, I grew spiritually and truly understood what it meant to believe that "I can do all things through Christ who strengthens me."

Finally, once your goal is realized, the sense of accomplishment you experience will give you the confidence to pursue other endeavors that you may not have attempted. When you attain your degree, license, or certification, you realize that you have the ability to do something great. You can reflect on the experiences you gained through the process of accomplishing your goal, and to help you accomplish everything necessary for you fulfill your purpose.

If you don't have family support or encouragement, it is necessary to develop a support system. You may be able to look to your local community for mentorship through sororities, youth athletic groups, or other organizations that focus on youth development. It may also help to consult your guidance counselor regarding school based clubs that may focus on career opportunities. Another option may be to seek out someone that is currently doing what you desire to do in the future, and ask if they would be willing to mentor you.

Most importantly, before you embark on the journey toward post-secondary education, make sure you consult God about your life's purpose and the direction that He would have you to take in fulfilling it. "Trust in the Lord with all your heart and do not lean on your own understanding; submit to Him in all your ways and He will make your path straight" **Proverbs 3:5-6.**

The above answers was submitted by Shadreka T. McIntosh, Personal Pharmacist, PhanrmAssist Care.

Q.   I feel very self-conscious around my friends. Most of them eat like pigs, yet never gain weight. I have always been bigger and I'm not sure what steps I should take to be fit, feel comfortable, and become physically productive. What advice can you give me? (**Negative Self Image**)

A.   **Feeling self-conscious around friends who can eat like pigs and still maintain their ideal** weight is a normal feeling. However, you have to keep in mind that everyone's genetics and metabolism are different. Some genetic traits and a certain metabolism can allow a person to eat all they want and still not gain weight. While on the other hand, some genetic traits and metabolism do not allow for such eating habits. If you desire to remain fit and feel comfortable around friends, it is good to maintain a physically fit and active lifestyle, proper exercise, and healthy eating habits. While some friends may be smaller, feeling comfortable around them comes with being confident in the skin you are in. Comfortability is maintained with your level of Confidence, and Confidence is Knowing Who You Are!

> *The above answer was submitted by Toya Felston, Co-Founder: FitSistaz Ft. Myers and independent business owner of Total Life Changes.*

Q.   What advice would you give a girl that does not fit society's definition of beauty, and thus feels ugly and unwanted? **(Negative Self Image)**

A.   **The mirror is simply a reflection…*of your mindset.***

When you look in the mirror you will see exactly what you are looking for.

Looking for pimples? You will find every single one of them. Instead, look for ways to lovingly give yourself the food and hygiene routine that your body is telling you it needs…and give thanks.

Looking for imperfections? You will find them. Instead, look for all the ways your body is properly functioning…and give thanks.

Looking for ugliness? You will find it. Instead, look for evidence of the fact that you are fearfully and wonderfully made…and give thanks.

Psalm 139:14 "I will offer You my grateful heart, for I am Your unique creation, filled with wonder and awe. You have approached even the smallest details with excellence; Your works are wonderful; I carry this knowledge deep within my soul." The Voice Bible Translation (VOICE)

Flaws, failures, flub-ups—yeah, they happen. Less than wonderful hair days, wishing something was different about your appearance, we've all had those thoughts. But, making them the of your focus is misdirected and discounts your **internal light and your unique personal design** granted to you by the Creator.

Ultimately, you are beautiful because you are created *by* and *in* the image of the Divine.

How comfortable are you with the skin, and soul, you're in? It may take some time for you to **shift from using the mirror as a weapon by which you inflict emotional wounds on yourself to using it as an *opportunity to exercise self-care, self-compassion, and validation*** of your unique design.

What if you ***obsessed about the things that make you unique, valuable, and worthy?***

Go to the mirror. Look deeply.

What is **truly beautiful** about you?

What is **right** about you?

What is **lovely** about you?

Beauty is holistic. Beauty is about all the parts of you— body, soul, and Spirit. You will increase your self-esteem by focusing on your positive qualities.

Do you have lovely feminine hands? Do you serve up awesome advice to whomever needs it? Can you take pictures in a way that helps us see Creation in a new and amazing light? What talents and skills do you uniquely express? How do you use your gifts in service to humanity? Think deeply about these things, and give thanks for them.

"Finally, brothers and sisters, fill your minds with beauty and truth. Meditate on whatever is honorable, whatever is right, whatever is pure, whatever is lovely, whatever is good, whatever is virtuous and praiseworthy." **Philippians 4:8 The Voice Bible Translation (VOICE)**

One of the most important things that can dictate the course your entire life is your own view of yourself. There is something about how we see ourselves that can be like a self-fulfilling prophecy.

For example, if we see ourselves as underserving of something in our lives, there is only a small chance that we will end up attaining it.

Furthermore, how we view ourselves can affect our relationships with others, and we may find ourselves continually in unsatisfying relationships that are either abusive or lacking in some fundamental way.

Feelings of nervousness, anxiety, and a pervasive sense of our own inadequacy are all things that can come along with having low self-esteem.

Just as having a weak view of self lends itself to all of the issues mentioned above, strengthening your self-view can lead to the positive outcomes in all areas of your life.

How can you strengthen your self-view and put unhappy feelings behind you and start living the life you were meant to live?

Turn those negative beliefs upside down. Those negative beliefs that you're not good enough have got to go!

You will increase your self-esteem by focusing on your positive qualities. You've got some—lots of them. Honor your positive qualities. This is not prideful or vain. This a humble gratefulness for what the Creator has endowed in you.

- Start by writing down the things that you can do well and examples of things that you've been successful at in the past.
- Make a brief list of the times when you have felt beautiful and displayed beautiful character.

- Make a list of your good and beneficial qualities.

You may not feel a difference right away, however, writing down these facts helps to challenge the assumptions that your negative beliefs are currently based upon.

Over time, you may notice that you feel more confident and that your self-view and self-esteem are slowly being strengthened.

You can overcome self-doubt and turn it into self-esteem with the power of your mindset. Think of your recent accomplishments and make mental notes of your past achievements.

Your self-confidence grows each time your make a healthy and positive choice in your life. Write down every time you make a positive choice. Keep these notes and lists in a place where you can see them, including your mirror, and meditate on the beauty you possess and the beauty you bring to the world.

You have the power to build a better personal world. You can replace **perceived** perfectionism with the reality of your beautiful worth and value and maximize what you do love about yourself.

By taking these steps, you'll be going a long way towards strengthening your self-esteem, and you will be well on the road toward feeling happy and confident in yourself, exactly the way you are.

You are an extraordinary soul with many positive aspects that make you a special part of God's design.

So, the next time you approach that mirror, what will you be looking for? Whatever it is, you will find it.

The above answer was submitted by LaShaun Collier, Small Business Strategist, Publishing Editor of Spirit, Substance and Style Magazine.

Q.   One of the most popular ways to communicate with my friends is through social media. What advice can you give me on safety, posting, and meeting new friends on different social media sites? **(Social Media)**

A.   Social media platforms are a wonderful way to network, connect, and receive helpful information. Unfortunately, social media can have some negative side effects. Here are some things to keep in mind to protect your safety and well-being:

First, consider when and where you are updating your social media following on your life events. Be cautious to share "vacation" pictures while you are on vacation. Otherwise, you run the risk of inviting unwanted guests to your home. You may also want to refrain from sharing posts that would "tipoff" strangers about where you live or go to school.

Second, only accept "connection requests" from people you know. If you receive a "connection request" from someone you don't know, but they seem to have a few mutual friends in common, simply reach out to a trusted mutual friend and ask about the person who is requesting to connect with you.

Third, before you post anything, ask yourself, "Is this something I would want my Grandmother/Family Member/Future Employer to see?" If the answer is no, it is probably best that you do not post or share the post. Remember, future employers have a way to look at your social media history. Even if you have privacy settings on your account, this doesn't stop your "friends" from copying or sharing information about you.

At the end of the day, it's better to post "life events" after they happen, and it's always a good idea to be on your best behavior at all times.

The above answer was submitted by Erica Castner Queen of Results Business Consulting, Breakthrough Coach.

Q.   I am very creative and innovative. I have so many ideas that can produce income and assist others. What advice can you give me about starting my own business? **(Entrepreneurship)**

A.   It's great to be creative and innovative and to have loads of ideas, but putting that energy to work for you is the next step. I suggest writing a plan for each business idea. The plan can be very simple when you start organizing your thoughts. Write down the product or service that you will provide, write down what makes your product or service different or unique, then start listing who will use your product or service—your target market. Is your target customer young, old, middle-aged, or any age? Be specific. Brainstorm with a mentor on how you can reach these target customers. Will it be through social media, channel marketing through another business, online or direct sales to friends, family, and the community?

I've been self-employed most of my life and it takes determination and stick-to-it-ness to thrive. Believe you can do it and make each day count.

My advice is to be organized, write down your goals, and find a mentor that has built a business and that can work as your advisor during your new venture. I've had many mentors along my path.

The above answer was submitted by E. Sue Huff of E. Sue Huff & Associates, Inc. – Marketing and Management Consulting, Naples, Florida.

Q. I was on an interview and was asked about how I give back to my community. I had no idea that community service was important. What makes it so important? **(Helping Others)**

A. Community service is a very selfless act. It demonstrates to others that there are causes that impact you other than personal goals and desires. Community Service is so important in shaping an individual's life. When young people give back to their community through volunteering or spreading awareness about a world issue, it helps them step out of familiar environments and expand their horizons. There are great benefits associated with Community Services such as skill development, leadership, decision making, and doing something great that will benefit someone in need. It also helps you to learn more about yourself and the causes that inspire you to invoke change and, most importantly, develop a sense of compassion and gratitude for what you have and for others.

The above answer was submitted by Barbara Melvin, CEO/Owner-BMR-Melvin Consulting.

Q. What age is appropriate for attraction to a male with consideration of being more than friends? How do you have the "I am ready to like boys" conversation with your parents? **(Dating)**

A. Well, Well, Well! Let me start off by saying that there is nothing wrong with liking boys or thinking they are cute. This feeling is very healthy and natural. It is imperative that before you act on those feelings, you create some rules for yourself:

- Never leave your parent or guardian in the dark when it comes to making serious decisions. They may not condone, allow, or be happy about your feeling, but they know what's best for you.

- Make sure you have not placed your desire for a boy over God, family, or school. You are at a young, tender age and trust me, boys will always be there. We tend to focus on what "will be" there and miss out on nurturing and prioritizing what's "already" there.

- Come up with some standards before ever establishing any relationship. Everyone needs a set of rules to assist them with maintaining healthy relationships. So, even if your parents say that you are too young to talk or date, ask them to help you create standards to help you when it's time.

- Never allow any friend, boy or what's popular on media cause to you to feel you that are centuries behind just because you are not allowed to approach, or have not yet been approached by, a boy.

- Parents release us when we prove ourselves trustworthy and responsible. Now is the time for you to make good choices so that when the time comes to have that conversation, you are ready for the responsibility and trust it takes.

- The worst thing you can do is lie or sneak behind your parents' backs. This will cause you to gain the boy you like for now, but lose the trust with your parents that you will need later.

The above answer was submitted by TaSheekia Pery Founder of Crowning Daughters for Success Enrichment Program, Girl Talk Host, Lee Pitts Live Talk Show.

Q.   I have been hearing about a lot of girls being kidnapped and used for sex. What is human trafficking, and how can I stay safe? **(Awareness/Safety)**

A.   Human Trafficking is Modern Day Slavery (Commercially Sexually Exploited Children, Forced Labor, Sex Trafficking, and Domestic Servitude). Sex trafficking is that in which a commercial sex act is induced by force, fraud, or coercion, or in which a person that is under the age of 18 years is induced in such act. Human Trafficking is also when a person's labor or service is obtained through force, fraud, or coercion for the purpose of involuntary servitude, peonage, debt bondage, or slavery.

You can stay safe by telling someone when you don't feel safe, not talking to strangers, and not giving your personal information. Don't make decisions under the influence or when being pressured, be aware when someone is making promises that are unrealistic, be aware of someone who is trying to befriend you too quickly and buys you gifts for no reason, be aware of an older person in an inappropriate relationship with a minor, and TELL, TELL, TELL.

10 Signs of Human Trafficking:

1. False IDs and lying about age
2. Bruising, injuries, branding tattoos, marks on body
3. Youth or adult with a very controlling companion
4. Individual restricted from contact with others by companion
5. Inconsistencies in story
6. Inability to make eye contact
7. Withdrawn or anxious behavior
8. Lack of knowledge about the community or whereabouts
9. Substance abuse

10. Youth reveals excessive absences or lack of enrollment in school

Human Trafficking SIGNS: www.humantraffickingawareness.org

The above answer was submitted by Karen Watson, MSW, Executive Director Our Mother's Home.

Q. I am around an adult male and he makes me feel uncomfortable. Some of the comments he makes are very inappropriate. What should I do? (**Awareness/Safety**)

A. Fear not, you have a direct line to God through your prayers. Utilize it. God is your shield and will be with thee at all times and in all situations. Do not ignore your alarm bells. Any inappropriate behavior unwanted by you is totally inappropriate for YOU. You are not powerless. Use action words and action to gain your power back. Note that you are extremely powerful by first acknowledging the fact that you have boundaries that no man should cross.

Know the meaning of the word "**Dis**"—express your **dis**likes. After doing so, if his behavior continues to escalate or become confrontational, disengage and disassociate yourself immediately. Do not become distracted by his compliments or over- friendliness. Keep in mind at all times that there is something wrong when an adult male displays inappropriate behavior and/or sexual attraction towards you. Confide in someone you trust. Start out by saying that you've noticed his inappropriate behaviors, and that it makes you feel very uncomfortable and disrespected whenever he disregards your boundaries and/or personal space .Leave out the Y in the word YOU. If you start to question yourself as to Y did I wear this dress, Y did I sit next to him, Y did I smile back at him. YYYYY.... Do not play the blame game; you're not to blame YOU for his inappropriate actions.

The above answer was submitted by Temple White-Scott, Non-Profit Organizer and Small Business Specialist.

Q.   How do I overcome the fear of being around people that seem different? **(Fear)**

A.   It is only natural to be afraid or uncomfortable when you are around people who are different from you. This difference can come in many forms such as your language, customs, the way in which you dress, where you live, the size and make-up of your family, your skin tone, your gender and sexual orientation, your religion and the way that you think (this is diversity in its simplest form).

To overcome this fear, I think it is very important that you (1) know who you are and (2) take the time to learn about others and to show love and compassion for them.

What is your culture and how does it impact the way that you think? What is your family heritage?

If you understand who you are and how your culture has affected you, it's easier to understand how it could affect anyone else or why it might be important to them. If you know who you are and are comfortable talking about your own culture, then you will become better at adapting to others and listening to them talk about theirs.

By knowing who you are, you gain self-confidence by knowing your strengths and weakness, and where you can and should make self-improvements.

When you meet new people, instead of focusing on your differences, focus on the ways in which you are alike. You will find that you have a lot in common, and a lot to learn.

Instead of focusing on yourself and how you are different, see this as an opportunity to learn about other cultures through their food, music, religion, and customs. This will make you not only wiser, but more likeable and engaging.

Even as you get older, you will find yourself in situations where you may feel like an outsider or the only one. When I find myself in this type of situation and that fear creeps in, I look around the room for someone who might appear to be lonely and isolated. I approach this person and start a conversation to make them feel welcomed and included. In other words, I take the attention off of myself and try to help that person because I know the fear that comes with being different. I do believe that when you give of yourself it is given back to you two-fold.

Dedicate time to knowing the beautiful and unique person that you are, and make time to learn about others. It is a life changing experience.

The above answer was submitted by Gail B. Williams, M.B.A., CDP, Chief Diversity Officer, Hodges University.

Q.   I love to swim and enjoy outdoor activities. I feel so self-conscious wearing tank tops and bathing suits because my parents will not allow me to shave. Please help me to help them understand!

A.   When I was a young girl around the age of 13, I went through this exact same thing. I began to grow hair on my legs, under my arms, and in my private area, but my grandmother was not very fond of me shaving. She said that women should never shave, no matter what. I realized that she didn't have hair on her legs like I did, so to her it was no big deal, but I let her know that it was a big deal to me. I felt like a man by having hair under my arms and on my legs. When I would dress out for gym, I would notice that most girls did not have hair like me and would just stare. That was pretty embarrassing, to say the least. When I asked one of my friends why she didn't have hair on her legs or under her arms, she said it was because she had started shaving. So, after coming home and just sitting down, having an open conversation, and expressing my feelings to my grandmother, she eventually allowed me to shave. She just wanted me to take the necessary precautions when shaving so that I wouldn't cut myself. So, my advice is to have an honest conversation with your parents about how you feel and explain the reason(s) why you think you should be allowed to shave.

This above answer was submitted by Precious Bennet.

Q.   I have made some poor choices and now my parents do not trust me. How can I regain their trust back? **(Family)**

A.   As a teenager, I had made some poor choices. As a result, I, too, lost the trust of my parents and loved ones. Therefore, I learned that when you lose the trust of your parents, family, and friends, it is very difficult to win it back. Well, here is some good news to your question. Trust is like a bank account that people make deposits into based on your character as a person of good reputation. That account of trust you have established with your parents should be considered very valuable. Your personal choices should be based on how much you value your parents' trust. Otherwise, you lose all the trust that they have placed in you; you empty that trust account you have gained to this point. To regain that trust account, you would have to be tested over time, so be consistent, truthful, reliable, and accountable. Your parents will observe how you go through various tests, such as following their rules and expectations. When your parents see that you stay steady, they will make a deposit into your trust account. Let me share some keys to remember—be a person of integrity and do what is right even when no one is watching. Prove your reliability so that your parents will place additional deposits into your account of trust. Trust holds a great value that you do not want to violate, and it says a lot about your character and your good reputation. Furthermore, trust and reputation is easier kept than regained.

The above answer was submitted by Rose Young, Youth Mentor/Certified Addiction Counselor and co-founder of SWFL Youth Empowerment Project.

Q. I feel like a total outcast. I have to take medication because of an emotional disorder. I don't like to tell people because I don't want anyone to think I am crazy. Can you give me some advice on how I can deal with this? **(Negative Feelings)**

A. In life, we all feel a little crazy at times and our emotions seem to go on a roller coaster. Many of us cry one minute and are happy the next, get frustrated, and sometimes just do not want to be bothered whether we are considered to have an emotional issue or not. Pretty funny, huh? However, some of us are so smart that our brains try to process more than they can handle at one time, and this causes our emotions to take over, and sometimes we don't know how to stop it and get refocused. So, to make sure that you are able to focus, be successful, and share your gift of knowledge with others, the medication is needed to slow your brain down so that it properly processes all of the information you need. It's like your central processing unit or computer. The computer can hold and process so many games, apps, documents, and codes. Sometimes, when the computer is not able to shut down or relax, it starts running hot, getting slow, and burning out. Then, some of us will get frustrated with it and bang on it while yelling, "This computer is crazy! Something is wrong with it!" Because the owner or you did not allow the computer to rest, it was operating on overload. Now, similar to your brain, the computer can hold a lot of information because it's way too smart. So, by providing it with virus protection software, it is kept from breaking down and can process everything in order for the users or you to get the information needed. This is the same as you taking medication to help regulate your emotions and how much knowledge you can retain to help others. Because you have the gift of being able to process a lot of information, it takes medication to slow your brain down in order for you to be able to process the information and spread your knowledge to the world. So, medication for you is the same as virus protection for your computer. If your brain or the computer does not get what it needs to prevent it from going haywire, then, yes, it may seem to be crazy. Think about this, when your cell phone, computer, or game acts up and prevents you from enjoying it, the first thing you do is put it to the side and play with something else until it gets fixed and you can enjoy it again. Right? And, since you know you do not like the feeling of being cast out or made to feel different or crazy, you should continue to take the medication so that everyone can continue to see the smart, intelligent, successful leader that you are. Everyone has problems controlling their emotions sometimes, but no one has to know that you take medicine unless you tell them.

The above answer submitted by Fayola Caines Master of Science, Mental Health Counseling.

Q.   I think my teacher hates me. She is always calling me out for something! How can I stand up for myself and maintain a positive relationship with her? **(Negative Feelings)**

A.   By the time you are in middle or high school, you have encountered many different teachers throughout the years. You have had teachers that you absolutely loved and some that you really couldn't stand. A teacher-student relationship is an extremely important factor in the success of your education. This relationship can encourage you to soar to educational heights or foster a dislike for school that changes your purpose and destiny in life. Not only should your teachers educate you, but they have the responsibility to address the social and emotional concerns that impact you as student. As a veteran teacher, I know that there are two kinds of students that we are more likely to call out for something: Students who never follow the rules and students who are not working up to their potential. So, before you approach your teacher, ask yourself what type of student you are. Once you have taken a personal inventory of your attitude and effort in this class, then it's time to talk to your teacher. Although a teacher is an authoritative figure at school, you still have the right to question your teacher when you have a concern.

The Word of God tells us in Deuteronomy 31:6, "Be strong and courageous. Do not be afraid or terrified because of them, for the LORD your God goes with you; He will never leave you nor forsake you." So, before you talk to your teacher, come against the spirit of fear and a confrontational attitude. Pray that God will be with you, give you favor, and that your teacher has a listening ear and an open heart. Go to your teacher in a respectful and responsible manner. Discuss with them your concerns and give specific examples. Allow your teacher the opportunity to address your concerns. As a team, come up with solutions and strategies to improve the area of concern. Conclude your meeting with an attitude of gratitude for the teacher taking time to discuss your concerns. Hopefully, this positive meeting will change how you feel about your teacher. If there is no change, then it is time to get your parents and/or school administrators involved, but always attempt to talk to your teacher before you take this final step. A teacher can respect and appreciate a student who takes the initiative to respectfully address a concern. Teachers love students who come to school to learn, try their very best, and follow school-wide expectations. Never ever ignore your feelings about a teacher. It is critical that they become a part of your village that will help you become a successful adult that strives to impact communities and change the world.

The above answer was submitted by Dr. Mia German, Founder of Dr. Mia's Learning Lab.

Q.   I sometimes feel alone and left out. It's hard to see the good when you are dealing with so much bad. How can I deal with these negative feelings? **(Negative Feelings)**

A.   My advice would be to listen to that quiet voice within you that so desperately wants to be heard by you, that voice that tells you, "I've got your back,." that voice that tells you, "I know you can make it," that voice that tells you that you are more than what you are surrounded by.

A. I want you to know that the negativity is going to be there, but you have to push through the negativity to get to your purpose. Begin to ask yourself better questions such as, "What is my purpose? Who can I help? What service can I provide?" Most of all, listen to that small voice inside that will answer these questions for you.

The above answer submitted by Ebony Simms, Author-Attitudes of Gratitude.

Q. Why is what I listen to and watch a major concern? Isn't media and music just entertainment? **(Pop Culture)**

A. What you listen to, and the images that you see, are very important. Most people do not understand that the mind is not fully developed until the age of 21. Your mind and senses are very impressionable and easily influenced by what you see and hear. We start mental habits and ways of thinking by observation. You may not act on the very thing you see or hear, however, what you see and hear does affect how you act. Our choices begin in the mind. We think on the action before we act on it. If all you have swarming through your mind is inappropriate images and words, it is a great chance that your actions will coincide. Not all music, TV shows, media, or entertainment is bad. We all like to laugh, enjoy an inspiring song, or view a great movie, and there is nothing wrong with that. It becomes wrong when it is insulting to God, has a negative influence, and causes you to mimic the wrong character. What we see and hear leaves an impression on how we think. How we think produces values. Our values birth choices. We have to safeguard our mind and free it from anything that will taint it. Think about the word Entertainment. The first word I notice is Enter, which means to go in. The second word I notice is Retain, which means to keep possession of. What goes in your mind is kept. If you are going to keep something, let it be positive, productive, and appropriate. I always try to compare what I watch and view to scripture.

The above answer was submitted by TaSheekia Perry, Founder of Crowning Daughters for Success Enrichment Program, Girl Talk Host on Lee Pitts Live Talk Show

Q.   What is beauty?

A.   Truthfully, beauty is not all that hard to find even though everyone is desperately searching. Ladies, just KNOW that you are beautiful. Believe it! Own it! Embrace it! Loving yourself is a must even though you are imperfect. If you permit yourself to be beautiful, any presentation you may choose is but one of your beauty's many expressions. After all, you are indeed God's beautiful expression. Most people think that wearing a revealing outfit to fit in brings about appreciation. It does not. It brings about inner conflict. Certainty will always breed certainty, and if you are certain that you are beautiful and brilliant, as a man, I am inspired to believe that WE can be beautiful together. I am born to appreciate beauty through you. This is my only way since God has given you power to birth all things. As a man, beauty is but an idea to me. I find you beautiful when beauty has ceased being an idea in my head and has become a certain reality within you.

The above answer was submitted by Earnest Graham Jr., President of Pro Player Insurance Group.

Please Note: These answers are for informational purposes only. The information provided by various individuals is not to be supplemented, replaced, or substituted for any legal, physiological, medical, and/or parental guidance of any sort. This information is not advice or direct remedies, and should not be treated as such. You should never delay seeking legal advice, disregard legal advice, seek medical attention, disregard medical attention, or commence or discontinue any legal action, medication, or medical action because of information in this journal.

The publisher and the author hereby disclaim any liability to any party for any loss, damages, or disruption caused by errors or omissions, whether such errors or omissions result from negligence, accident, or any other cause. The publisher and the author have made every attempt to safeguard that the information in this journal was correct at the time of press.

Dressing My Inner Beauty Journal Page
How I Dressed My Inner Beauty Today

Dressing My Inner Beauty

Celebrating the Beauty of My Inner Beauty is the Latest Fashion!

Inner Beauty Matters the Most

Welcome to a Surprise Celebration! What I love the most about this type of Celebration is that the special occasion is You! Many times in life, it is so easy to get sidetracked with the images promoted, the beauty messages we hear, and comparisons we make between ourselves and others. This has a major effect on how we view and feel about ourselves. Much of what you see throughout media are unrealistic expectations about beauty, yet everyone seems to strive for it. We want you to be encouraged by your inner beauty and celebrate it proudly. When I speak about beauty, I am not talking about facial features and body types. I am speaking on a beauty that lasts- **your Inner Beauty**. I have worked with teen girls for over 10 years. The greatest complaint about how they feel about themselves is, "I am TOOOOOO". "I am too short! I am too skinny! I am too dark! My cheeks are too chubby!" Growing up, I was also affected by those **terrible toos**. Remember we talked about these. It is way too easy to focus on those "terrible toos". Remember to change your self-talk to focus on your strengths. I thought I was too short. I felt like a dwarf every time I stood next to my taller peers. I got over the too-short syndrome when I discovered that my best friend felt that she was too tall. We laughed about what we thought was awful, and embraced what we could not change. I felt good about myself until I started playing the comparison game. This mind game causes you to look at someone else and admire their features while downplaying yours. I was losing. Yes, every time I compared myself to someone else, I would forget what was so special about me. This would cause me to speak more negatively or highlight my flaws. I would have to constantly remind myself that there is no other person that can beat me at being me. So, I decided to take myself out of that game. Listen, it is ok to look at someone and admire them, but **never** compare. Many girls have conformed to the wrong mindset and idea about what it is to be beautiful. Many don't understand that what seems different and awkward to them is what makes them special and beautiful to others.

In high school, I learned that Inner Beauty was the best kind of beauty. I was well liked, popular, and a part of many extracurricular activities. My senior year, I decided to run for Homecoming Queen. This was a competition in which the whole school could vote. Prior to running, I remember my younger peers approaching me and wanting to befriend me. Now, it was not considered cool to hang out with the underdogs, but I did. I talked to them, laughed with them, and treated a lot of them like little siblings. My classmates teased me sometimes because I truly desired to make the lower classmen feel accepted. The voting opened up, and I had some tough competition. Imagine every pretty, smart, and well-liked girl running for the same title. A teacher who was head of the Homecoming Activities pulled me aside at the close of the votes. He shared that it was a very close race between my peers and me. He stated that I would have to wait until the great reveal "Homecoming Game" to hear results, but asked, "How did you get 90% of all underclassmen votes?" The underclassmen, posted my signs, encouraged their friends to vote for me, and supported me. They always talked about how I never allowed my looks to override being kind and genuine. This meant a lot to me, and I always think back on this experience when I deal with people.

I get many compliments, but the greatest compliments are not about my looks or what I'm wearing. They are about my character and the way I treat people. If you are into awards shows or events that recognize people, you will notice that the most popular awards many receive are for great character, academic achievements, and certificates of appreciation, talent, and much more, not looks. **These are all awards that recognize what truly makes someone beautiful.**

We want to celebrate all of those inwardly beautiful qualities that bring out the best you. It is imperative that you understand and embrace the total essence of who you are! **When you establish unconditional self-love and value yourself, other relationships will benefit.** Many people wait for a certain day, achievement, or event to celebrate. You can celebrate being you daily by sharing your inner gifts of love, service, compassion, or your best inner quality with those around you.

What exactly does it mean to value yourself? Does it mean to think you are better than everyone else? Does it mean to think that you know it all? Absolutely not! To value yourself is the most crucial aspect of your life. You are of importance to God! This is why He gifted the world with you. So, it is your obligation to embrace this importance and never allow anyone to undermine the great gift you are. Valuing yourself is all about appreciating yourself enough to make healthy decisions, take care of your wellbeing, and filter that same love to others. **We can't expect anyone to love and respect us if we have not made that our number one rule for ourselves.** It's equivalent to the Golden Rule, which is one of our most important commandments from God—treat others how you want to be treated. When we love, respect, and value ourselves, this shows how we want to be treated. In return, we should treat others the same way. When we do not recognize the value we have because of Christ's blessings, we tend to devalue, overlook, and treat others poorly. I've noticed that most bullies are not evil people; they are people who do not value themselves, so they do not see value in other people.

I have come up with some **Inner Beauty Tips** that will assist you in Celebrating Daily:

- Look at Inner Beauty as if it were a Gift. When someone gives you a beautiful box dressed up in colorful wrappings, you admire the outward dressing, but what you really want is the gift inside. This is the exact same way you should think of yourself. Be that FAB girl you are, and don't miss the gift that resides within.

- Never judge a person solely on his/her outer wrapping. You may miss out on a great friend or an awesome connection because of this.

- Inner Beauty is the best kind of Beauty because it causes people to connect with you authentically. When people connect with you because of what you have or the way you look, it is easy for that person to push you aside for someone they feel looks better or has more.

- Self-Love is actually not solely about you. It is about building a healthy awareness, love, and appreciation for yourself so that you can treat others the right way and signal to others the way you want to be treated.

Your outward gift-wrapping may not look like everybody else's wrapping. Your wrapping may be a different color, shape, or size. However, there is yet a gift on the inside of you! Your personality, character, standards, and values are a gift to yourself and to others. As your relationship with Christ blossoms, your character will blossom and your relationships will be on a winning streak. The outward image that we see of others is the wrapping. It cannot assist when someone needs encouraging words, a helping hand, or a good friend.

Image and the way we look are important. We make good or poor impressions because of the way we present our total selves. However, the true gift is the Inner You. **One wisdom nugget I share with my participants is that looks can only get you so far; character and those awesome inner qualities will take you the rest of the way.**

After each chapter, you have been challenged to write about how you dressed your Inner Beauty according to the lesson topic. I want to challenge you above that. I know you can do it, and feel free to invite your family and friends to join the challenge with you. Help the CDFS program spread the message about Inner Beauty. Continue writing on the journal pages that will be provided. Write daily about how you dress your Inner Beauty. For example, I dressed my Inner Beauty today by sharing and caring for my grandmother who was sick. It is also "No Makeup Tuesday". Since 2014, I have taken off my makeup to support the Beauty Beyond the Outer Project. Yes!!! No makeup on Tuesdays for me and many of my social media friends, family, and coworkers. We want the world to embrace that girls are more than cosmetics, features, and figures. We are beautiful from the Inside and Out. We would love to hear some of your Inner Beauty Journal writings, and for those of you that are old enough and have parental permission to wear makeup, send us those no makeup photos! I am celebrating you, cheering for you, and declaring that the absolute best will manifest through You! **Let the Inner Beauty Celebration and Challenge begin! Share your Inner Beauty experiences at Crowningdaughters@gmail.com**

Dressing My Inner Beauty Journal Page
How I Dressed My Inner Beauty Today

_____

_____

_____

_____

_____

_____

_____

_____

_____

_____

_____

_____

_____

_____

_____

_____

_____

_____

_____

Monday   Tuesday   Wednesday   Thursday   Friday   Saturday   Sunday

Dressing My Inner Beauty
I am now Inner Beauty Ready!

Hello, Beautiful!

Thank you so much for investing the time, energy, and work to ensure you are equipped for the amazing journey ahead of you. The Information, Times of Reflection, Writings and TaSheekia's Tidbits will assist you for the now and for the later. Along this journey, there will be times you feel as if you can't do it or people will tell you that you can't do it, but I say you can do all things through Christ Jesus. As you complete this final journal topic, determine to never quit on yourself, always ask for help, and continue to be as beautiful inwardly as you are outwardly. You are an amazing gift, but the most amazing aspect of you is hidden until you reveal it to others. I know media is still promoting unrealistic images for young girls to live up to, peers are still being impressed by the outward, and the most popular is still the one that has all the boys whispering. Many things may not have changed since you started this journal. However, **you** have changed, and it is your time to show the world what it means to have **Confidence Without Compromise!** Enjoy this the next chapter in your life. Treat yourself to an Inner Beauty Party. Ask a teacher, mentor, parent or youth pastor to help you plan something as intimate as two friends, or something as big as an "Inner Beauty" party with many friends. One more thing, use the remaining Journal pages to continue journaling your Inner Beauty Experience. It has been noted that it takes about 21 days to break a habit. I'm giving you a bonus 21 pages to continue your daily Inner Beauty Reflections. **You did it, and I am proud of you!**

TaSheekia

Date:_____

Dressing My Inner Beauty Journal Page
How I Dressed My Inner Beauty Today

_____

_____

_____

_____

_____

_____

_____

_____

_____

_____

_____

_____

_____

_____

_____

_____

_____

_____

Monday   Tuesday   Wednesday   Thursday   Friday   Saturday   Sunday

Dressing My Inner Beauty Journal Page
How I Dressed My Inner Beauty Today

_____

_____

_____

_____

_____

_____

_____

_____

_____

_____

_____

_____

_____

_____

_____

_____

_____

_____

Monday   Tuesday   Wednesday   Thursday   Friday   Saturday   Sunday

Dressing My Inner Beauty Journal Page
How I Dressed My Inner Beauty Today

Date:_____

Dressing My Inner Beauty Journal Page
How I Dressed My Inner Beauty Today

_____

_____

_____

_____

_____

_____

_____

_____

_____

_____

_____

_____

_____

_____

_____

_____

_____

_____

Monday   Tuesday   Wednesday   Thursday   Friday   Saturday   Sunday

Date:_____

Dressing My Inner Beauty Journal Page
How I Dressed My Inner Beauty Today

_____

_____

_____

_____

_____

_____

_____

_____

_____

_____

_____

_____

_____

_____

_____

_____

_____

_____

_____

_____

Dressing My Inner Beauty Journal Page
How I Dressed My Inner Beauty Today

_____

_____

_____

_____

_____

_____

_____

_____

_____

_____

_____

_____

_____

_____

_____

_____

_____

_____

Monday   Tuesday   Wednesday   Thursday   Friday   Saturday   Sunday

Date:_____

Dressing My Inner Beauty Journal Page
How I Dressed My Inner Beauty Today

Date:_____

Dressing My Inner Beauty Journal Page
How I Dressed My Inner Beauty Today

_____

_____

_____

_____

_____

_____

_____

_____

_____

_____

_____

_____

_____

_____

_____

_____

_____

Monday   Tuesday   Wednesday   Thursday   Friday   Saturday   Sunday

Dressing My Inner Beauty Journal Page
How I Dressed My Inner Beauty Today

Date:_____

Dressing My Inner Beauty Journal Page
How I Dressed My Inner Beauty Today

_____

_____

_____

_____

_____

_____

_____

_____

_____

_____

_____

_____

_____

_____

_____

_____

_____

Monday   Tuesday   Wednesday   Thursday   Friday   Saturday   Sunday

Dressing My Inner Beauty Journal Page
How I Dressed My Inner Beauty Today

_____

_____

_____

_____

_____

_____

_____

_____

_____

_____

_____

_____

_____

_____

_____

_____

_____

_____

Monday   Tuesday   Wednesday   Thursday   Friday   Saturday   Sunday

Dressing My Inner Beauty Journal Page
How I Dressed My Inner Beauty Today

_____

_____

_____

_____

_____

_____

_____

_____

_____

_____

_____

_____

_____

_____

_____

_____

_____

_____

Monday   Tuesday   Wednesday   Thursday   Friday   Saturday   Sunday

Dressing My Inner Beauty Journal Page
How I Dressed My Inner Beauty Today

_____

_____

_____

_____

_____

_____

_____

_____

_____

_____

_____

_____

_____

_____

_____

_____

_____

_____

_____

_____

_____

Date:_____

Dressing My Inner Beauty Journal Page
How I Dressed My Inner Beauty Today

_____

_____

_____

_____

_____

_____

_____

_____

_____

_____

_____

_____

_____

_____

_____

_____

_____

_____

_____

_____

_____

Monday   Tuesday   Wednesday   Thursday   Friday   Saturday   Sunday

Dressing My Inner Beauty Journal Page
How I Dressed My Inner Beauty Today

_____

_____

_____

_____

_____

_____

_____

_____

_____

_____

_____

_____

_____

_____

_____

_____

_____

_____

_____

Monday   Tuesday   Wednesday   Thursday   Friday   Saturday   Sunday

Date:_____

Dressing My Inner Beauty Journal Page
How I Dressed My Inner Beauty Today

_____

_____

_____

_____

_____

_____

_____

_____

_____

_____

_____

_____

_____

_____

_____

_____

_____

_____

_____

_____

Monday   Tuesday   Wednesday   Thursday   Friday   Saturday   Sunday

Dressing My Inner Beauty Journal Page
How I Dressed My Inner Beauty Today

_____

_____

_____

_____

_____

_____

_____

_____

_____

_____

_____

_____

_____

_____

_____

_____

_____

_____

_____

_____

_____

Monday   Tuesday   Wednesday   Thursday   Friday   Saturday   Sunday

Dressing My Inner Beauty Journal Page
How I Dressed My Inner Beauty Today

_____

_____

_____

_____

_____

_____

_____

_____

_____

_____

_____

_____

_____

_____

_____

_____

_____

_____

_____

_____

_____

Dressing My Inner Beauty Journal Page
How I Dressed My Inner Beauty Today

_____

_____

_____

_____

_____

_____

_____

_____

_____

_____

_____

_____

_____

_____

_____

_____

_____

_____

_____

Dressing My Inner Beauty Journal Page
How I Dressed My Inner Beauty Today

_____

_____

_____

_____

_____

_____

_____

_____

_____

_____

_____

_____

_____

_____

_____

_____

_____

_____

_____

_____

Monday   Tuesday   Wednesday   Thursday   Friday   Saturday   Sunday

Dressing My Inner Beauty Journal Page
How I Dressed My Inner Beauty Today

70798898R00097

Made in the USA
San Bernardino, CA
08 March 2018